Vintage Knits *for* Babies

Vintage Knits
for Babies

More than **30** patterns for timeless
clothes and toys (0–18 months)

RITA TAYLOR

photography by Polly Wreford

jacqui
small

First published in 2015 by
Jacqui Small LLP
An imprint of Aurum Press Ltd
74–77 White Lion Street
London N1 9PF

ISBN: 978 1 909342 81 1

A catalogue record for this book is
available from the British Library.

2017 2016 2015
10 9 8 7 6 5 4 3 2 1

Printed in China

Publisher Jacqui Small
Designer and Art Director Sarah Rock
Commissioning and Project Editor Zia Mattocks
Technical Editor Linda McCreadie
Stylist Isabel de Cordova
Senior Editors Claire Chandler and Eszter Karpati
Editorial Assistant Alexandra Labbe Thompson
Production Maeve Healy

Additional photography Deirdre Rooney: pages 3, 27,
28, 41 top right, 41 bottom, 44 top left, 44 right, 63, 66,
70 top left, 70 right, 73, 79, 81, 91, 92, 93, 109, 119, 121,
123, 129, 131, 137, 138, 141 bottom, 142

Contents

Introduction

Until the mid-nineteenth century babies were dressed in a layer of underclothing, such as a vest or bodice of wool or linen with a long petticoat, and then swaddled – wrapped tightly in a blanket or cover, which pinned their arms to their sides and kept their legs straight. The swaddling would be removed from time to time to allow the baby to crawl about in its underclothes.

The only time babies wore loose clothing was when they were christened. Then they were dressed in a long robe, which was either made entirely of lacy stitches or trimmed with lace. The amount of lace knitting and the length of the skirt denoted the social status of the baby and its family.

When babies were taken out of doors, on top of their other layers of clothing, they were wrapped in a lacy shawl, often with a hood, known as a carrying shawl. Again, the size of the shawl signified status. During the middle of the eighteenth century, when Queen Victoria made prams (buggies) fashionable, the pram suit, comprising a matching set of leggings, coat, mittens and bonnet, replaced the carrying shawl. As ideas about the healthiest way to dress babies changed during the twentieth century, less-restrictive clothing, such as rompers and dresses, became widespread.

For this book I have looked at pictures and patterns typical of the type of clothing worn in the early part of the twentieth century. I have used these as inspiration, but altered and updated them to knit in some of the many luxurious modern yarns that are available. The oldest design is for the moss-stitch (seed-stitch) coat and bobble hat (see page 120), which is pre-1920; the newest is for the dress and bolero (see page 106), which were essential clothing for a 1950s girl. The other designs are mainly based on those from the 1930s and 1940s, but the styles are timeless, and I hope you will enjoy knitting them and seeing your baby wearing them.

'Come to the Christening'

Beautiful christening outfits

A christening was always a very special occasion for babies and their parents. It called for something even better than 'Sunday best', and the patterns for christening gowns often feature all-over lace or an elaborate lace trim. Boys and girls alike wore dresses with a very long, flowing skirt, falling from a short bodice, as in the traditional long dress (see page 10). While this style has remained popular, other designs, such as the short dress (see opposite and page 16), the two-piece outfit for boys (see page 26) or the lacy jacket set (see page 20), have come in vogue. Matching bootees could also be made, and the whole ensemble could be topped with a carrying shawl (see page 24).

SIZE
To fit 0–12 months (one size)

FINISHED MEASUREMENTS
Dress: Actual chest size 61cm/24in **Length to back neck** 66cm/26in
Sleeves 17cm/6½in
Bonnet: Crown to brim 13cm/5in **Circumference** 33cm/13in
Mittens: Length 11cm/4½in **Circumference** 15cm/6in

MATERIALS
Yarn Alpaca Select 4 ply (100% alpaca, 167m/183yd): 6 x 50g/1¾oz balls shade Natural 001
Needles 1 pair needles size 3.25mm (US3), 1 pair needles size 2.75mm (US2), 1 stitch holder
Notions 4 buttons, 1cm/⅜in diameter; 1m/39in thin shirring elastic for sleeves; 2m/2yd of ribbon, 2cm/1in wide

TENSION (GAUGE)
26 sts and 32 rows measure 10cm/4in over St st on 3.25mm (US3) needles (or size needed to obtain given tension/gauge)

'Daisy' Long Christening Dress Set

Victorian christening gowns were works of art, passed down through generations as family heirlooms. Worn by both boys and girls, they were similar in style to this dress, with a short yoke and long, flowing skirt, and were usually made of silk and trimmed with lace. This version, in soft alpaca, is reminiscent of the lacy christening dresses of that period and also has a matching bonnet and mittens.

DRESS
Pattern for hem
Odd rows 1–17: K1, yo, p5, p3tog, *p5, yo, k1, yo, p5, p3tog; rep from * 10 times, p5, yo, k1.

Even rows 2–44: Purl.

Row 19: K1, yo, ssk, yo, p3, p3tog, *p3, yo, k2tog, yo, k1, yo, ssk, yo, p3, p3tog; rep from * 10 times, p3, yo, k2tog, yo, k1.

Row 21: K1, yo, k1, ssk, yo, p2, p3tog, *p2, yo, k2tog, [k1, yo] twice, k1, ssk, yo, p2, p3tog; rep from * 10 times, p2, yo, k2tog, k1, yo, k1.

Row 23: K1, yo, k2, ssk, yo, p1, p3tog, *p1, yo, k2tog, k2, yo, k1, yo, k2, ssk, yo, p1, p3tog; rep from * 10 times, p1, yo, k2tog, k2, yo, k1.

Row 25: K1, yo, k3, ssk, yo, sk2po, *yo, k2tog, k3, yo, k1, yo, k3, ssk, yo, sk2po; rep from * 10 times, yo, k2tog, k3, yo, k1.

Row 27: K4, k2tog, yo, k2, *k1, yo, ssk, k7, k2tog, yo, k2; rep from * 10 times, k1, yo, ssk, k4.

Row 29: K3, k2tog, yo, k3, *k2, yo, ssk, k5, k2tog, yo, k3; rep from * 10 times, k2, yo, ssk, k3.

Row 31: K2, k2tog, yo, k4, *k3, yo, ssk, k3, k2tog, yo, k4; rep from * 10 times, k3, yo, ssk, k2.

Row 33: K1, k2tog, yo, k3, yo, sk2po, *yo, k3, yo, ssk, k1, k2tog, yo, k3, yo, sk2po; rep from * 10 times, yo, k3, yo, ssk, k1.

Row 35: K1, yo, ssk, k1, k2tog, yo, k2, *k1, yo, ssk, k2, yo, sk2po, yo, k2, k2tog, yo, k2; rep from * 10 times, k1, yo, ssk, k1, k2tog, yo, k1.

Row 37: K3, k2tog, yo, k3, *k2, yo, ssk, k5, k2tog, yo, k3; rep from * 10 times, k2, yo, ssk, k3.

Row 39: K2, k2tog, yo, k4, *k3, yo, ssk, k3, k2tog, yo, k4; rep from * 10 times, k3, yo, ssk, k2.

Row 41: K1, k2tog, yo, k5, *k4, yo, ssk, k1, k2tog, yo, k5; rep from * 10 times, k4, yo, ssk, k1.

Row 43: K1, ssk, k3, sk2po, *k4, yo, sk2po, yo, k4, sk2po; rep from * 10 times, k4, yo, k2tog.

Front

Using 3.25mm (US3) needles, cast on 155 sts and work in patt for hem for 44 rows. *(132 sts)*

Rows 45–47: Knit.

Row 48: Purl.

Next row (RS, dec row): *K5, sk2po, k4; rep from * to end. *(110 sts)*

Begin skirt pattern

Row 1: K7, *k2tog, yo, k3, yo, ssk, k3; rep from * to last 3 sts, k3.

Rows 2 and 4: Purl.

Row 3: K9, *yo, sk2po, yo, k7; rep from * to last st, k1.

Row 5: Knit.
Row 6: Purl.
Cont in patt as set until work measures 56cm/22in, ending after a WS row.

Shape armholes

Cast (bind) off 6 sts at beg of next 2 rows. *(98 sts)*
Dec 1 st at each end of next 3 rows and foll 3 alt rows. *(86 sts)*
Next row (WS): Purl.
Next row (RS): Purl.
Next row (dec row): K4, [k2tog] to last 4 sts, k4. *(47 sts)*
Next row (WS): Knit.
Cont in St st, beg with a knit row, until work measures 6cm/2¼in from beg of armhole shaping.

Shape neck

Next row: K17, k13 and leave these 13 sts on a holder, k17.
Working on last set of sts (right neck), dec 1 st at neck edge of next 4 rows. *(13 sts)*
Cont without shaping until work measures 9cm/3½in from armhole, ending after a WS row.
Work 7 rows garter st (knit every row), making buttonholes in 5th row as follows:
K3, [yo, k2tog, k3] twice.
Cast (bind) off.

Returning to sts for other shoulder, rejoin yarn to WS and complete to match.

Back

Work as for front until armholes measure 10cm/4in (omitting neckline shaping). *(47 sts)*

Work 4 more rows St st.
Cast (bind) off 13 sts at beg of next 2 rows. *(21 sts)*
Next 4 rows: Knit.
Work picot cast-off (bind-off) as follows:
Next row (RS): Cast (bind) off 3 sts, *slip last st back onto LH needle, cast on 2 sts, cast (bind) off 6 sts; rep from * to end.

Sleeves (make 2)

Using 2.75mm (US2) needles, cast on 61 sts and knit 4 rows.
Change to 3.25mm (US3) needles and work 6 rows St st.
Next row (eyelet row): K1, [yo, k2tog, K1] to end.
Cont in St st until sleeve measures 17cm/6½in.

Shape top

Cast (bind) off 6 sts at beg of next 2 rows. *(49 sts)*
Work 8 rows without shaping.
Dec 1 st at each end of next and every alt row until 39 sts rem.
Dec 1 st at each end of every row until 33 sts rem.
Cast (bind) off, working [k3tog] across row.

Front neckband

With RS facing, pick up and knit 11 sts down left side of neck, knit 13 sts from stitch holder, pick up and knit 11 sts along right side of neck.
Next 3 rows: Knit.
Work picot cast-off (bind-off) as follows:
Next row (RS): Cast (bind) off 3 sts, *slip last st back onto LH needle, cast on 2 sts, cast (bind) off 6 sts; rep from * to end.

Finishing

Set in sleeves, then sew up side and sleeve seams.
Sew on buttons at shoulders.
Weave in all ends.
Block or press carefully as given on page 142.
Thread elastic through eyelets to gather sleeves.

BONNET

Using 3.25mm (US3) needles, cast on 71 sts and purl 1 row.
Row 1 (RS): P8, *yo, p5, p3tog, p5, yo, p1; rep from * to last 7 sts, p7.
Row 2 (WS): Purl.
Rep these 2 rows 5 times more.
Next 2 rows: Purl.

Work lace pattern

Row 1: K7 *k2tog, yo, k3, yo, ssk, k3; rep from * to last 4 sts, k4.
Rows 2, 4 and 6: K4, purl to last 4 sts, k4.
Row 3: K9, *yo, sk2po, yo, k7; rep from * to last 2 sts, k2.
Row 5: Knit.

Shape crown

Row 1: *K8, k2tog; rep from * to last st, k1. *(64 sts)*
Row 2 and alt rows: Knit.
Row 3: *K7, k2tog; rep from * to last st, k1. *(57 sts)*
Row 5: *K6, k2tog; rep from * to last st, k1. *(50 sts)*
Row 7: *K5, k2tog; rep from * to last st, k1. *(43 sts)*
Cont dec on alt rows with one stitch less between decreases each time until 22 sts rem.
Next row: K2tog to end.
(11 sts)

'Daisy' Long Christening Dress Set

LACE PATTERN CHART

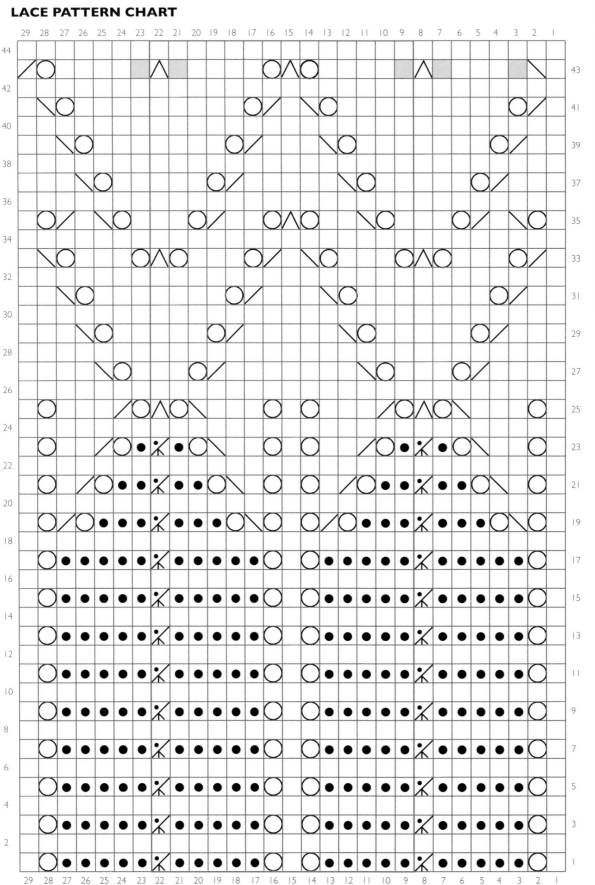

KEY

☐	RS: knit WS: purl
●	RS: purl WS: knit
○	RS: yo WS: yo
☐	repeat
╱	RS: k2tog WS: p2tog
╲	RS: ssk WS: p2tog tbl
╱╲	RS: sk2po WS: sl 1 wyif, p2tog tbl, psso
☐	repeat
✕	RS: p3tog WS: k3tog
▨	no stitch

Break yarn, thread through rem sts, draw up and fasten off.

Finishing

Sew up back seam, leaving a 9cm/ 3½in opening.
Sew ribbon to both front edges.
Weave in all ends.
Block or press carefully as given on page 142, if required.

MITTENS (MAKE 2)

Using 3.25mm (US3) needles, cast on 43 sts and purl 1 row.

Row 1 (RS): P2tog, p5, *yo, p1, yo, p5, p3tog, p5; rep from * to last 8 sts, yo, p1, yo, p5, p2tog.

Row 2 (WS): Purl.

Rep these 2 rows 4 times more.

Row 11: Knit.

Row 12: Purl.

Rep these 2 rows once more.

Next row (eyelet row): K1, [yo, k2tog, k1] to end.

Cont in St st for 5cm/2in.

Next row: K2, [k2tog, k4] 6 times, k2tog, k3. *(36 sts)*

Next row: Purl.

Shape top

Row 1: [K1, ssk, k12, k2tog, k1] twice. *(32 sts)*

Rows 2 and 4: Purl.

Row 3: [K1, ssk, k10, k2tog, k1] twice. *(28 sts)*

Row 5: [K1, ssk, k8, k2tog, k1] twice. *(24 sts)*

Cast (bind) off.

Finishing

Fold mittens in half and sew seam.
Weave in all ends.
Thread ribbon through eyelet holes and tie in a bow.

~15~

'Daisy' Long Christening Dress Set

SIZE
To fit 6–12 months

FINISHED MEASUREMENTS
Dress: Chest 48cm/22in (can be gathered with ribbon at the chest for a younger baby) **Length (to back neck)** 38cm/15in **Sleeves** 7.5cm/3in
Bonnet: Crown to brim 12.5cm/5in **Circumference** 33cm/13in

MATERIALS
Yarn Debbie Bliss Baby Cashmerino (55% wool, 33% microfibre, 12% cashmere, 125m/137yd): 4 x 50g/1¾oz balls shade 100 White
Needles 1 pair needles size 3.75mm (US5), 1 pair needles size 3mm (US2–3), 1 crochet hook size 3.5mm (USE/4), 3 stitch holders
Notions 3 buttons, 7mm/¼in diameter; 1m/1yd ribbon, approx 1cm/⅜in wide

TENSION (GAUGE)
24 sts and 30 rows measure 10cm/4in over St st on 3.75mm (US5) needles
(or size needed to obtain given tension/gauge)

'Chamomile' Short Christening Dress & Bonnet

Early in the twentieth century christening dresses became a little less elaborate, although they were still more decorative than everyday dresses and were trimmed with ribbons and lace. Short christening dresses are particularly suitable for babies who are crawling or starting to walk, and this one is simple enough to work for other occasions if knitted in a colour. I couldn't find a pattern for a short knitted christening dress from before 1950, so I designed this one from scratch. The dress still has a touch of lace with its interlinked hearts at the hem, to take it out of the everyday, but the little bonnet is plain, with a simple flower to add a touch of charm.

DRESS
Hearts pattern
Row 1: K1, *p1, k5, yo, sk2po, yo, k5, p1, k1; rep from * 6 times to end.
Row 2 and alt rows: Purl.
Row 3: K1, *p1, k3, k2tog, yo, k3, yo, ssk, k3, p1, k1; rep from * 6 times to end.
Row 5: K1, *p1, k2, k2tog, yo, k5, yo, ssk, k2, p1, k1; rep from * 6 times to end.
Row 7: K1, *p1, k1, k2tog, yo, k7, yo, ssk, k1, p1, k1; rep from * 6 times to end.
Row 9: K1, *p1, k2tog, yo, k3, yo, sk2po, yo, k3, yo, ssk, p1, k1; rep from * 6 times to end.
Row 11: K1, *p1, k2, yo, k3tog, yo, k3, yo, k3tog, yo, k2, p1, k1; rep from * 6 times to end.
Row 13: K1, *p1, k2, k2tog, yo, k5, yo,

ssk, k2, p1, k1; rep from * 6 times to end.
Row 15: K1, *p1, k1, k2tog, yo, k7, yo, ssk, k1, p1, k1; rep from * 6 times to end.
Row 16: Purl.

Back

Using 3.75mm (US5) needles, cast on 97 sts.
Rows 1 and 2: Knit.
Rows 3 and 4: K2, *yo, k2tog; rep from * to last st, k1.
Rows 5–7: Knit.
Row 8: Purl.
(Rows 1–6 form the hem patt.)

Work rows 1–16 of hearts patt, then rows 9–16 again, followed by rows 9–12 once more.

Next row (RS): K1, *p1, K13, p1, k1; rep from * to end.
Next row: Purl.
Rep these 2 rows twice more.
Row 9: K1, *p1, ssk, k9, k2tog, p1, k1; rep from * to end. (*85 sts*)
Row 10: Purl.
Work 8 rows in established patt without further decreases.
Row 19: K1, *p1, ssk, k7, k2tog, p1, k1; rep from * to end. (*73 sts*)
Cont in patt as set without further shaping until work measures 28cm/11in from beg.

Shape armhole

Cast (bind) off 2 sts at beg of next 2 rows. (*69 sts*)
Dec 1 st at each end of next and foll 2 alt rows. (*63 sts*)
Dec for yoke as follows:
Next row (RS): K2, sk2po, k1, *p1, k1, p1, k3, sk2po, k3; rep from * to last 9 sts, p1, k1, p1, k3, sk2po, k2. (*51 sts*)

Eyelets

Work rows 2–6 as for hem.

Back opening

Row 1: K27 and slip rem 24 sts onto a holder for other side, turn.
Row 2: K3, p to end.
Rep these 2 rows until armhole measures 10cm/4in, finishing at the armhole edge.

Shape shoulder

Cast (bind) off 6 sts at beg of next row, and 5 sts at beg of foll alt row. (*16 sts*)
Break yarn and leave rem 16 sts on a holder for back of neck.

Return to sts for left side:
Slip sts from holder back onto a needle and, with RS facing, cast on 3 sts.
Keeping the 3 sts at opening in garter st, work to match first side, making [yo, k2tog] buttonholes on 9th and foll 10th rows.

Front

Work as for back until armhole measures 6cm/2½in, ending with a WS row.

Shape neck

Next row (RS): K19, k13 and slip these 13 sts onto a holder, k19.
Cont to work on the last set of 19 sts for the right neck:
Next row: P16, p2tog, p1. (*18 sts*)
Next row: K1, ssk, k to end. (*17 sts*)
Cont dec at neck edge on every row until 11 sts rem.
Cont without shaping until work measures the same as back to beg of shoulder shaping.
Next row (WS): Cast (bind) off 6 sts at beg of next row, and 5 sts on foll alt row.
With WS facing, rejoin yarn to rem 19 sts of left side of neck and work to match, reversing shaping.
Join shoulder seams.

Neckline

Using 3mm (US2–3) needles and starting at left back neck edge:
Next row (RS): [K2, yo, k2tog, k12] from holder, pick up and knit 15 sts down left front neck, k13 from holder, pick up and knit 15 sts up right front neck and k16 from right back holder. (*75 sts*)
Work rows 2–5 in hem patt, but keeping 3 sts at beg, and end in garter st.
Cast (bind) off.

Sleeves (make 2)

Using 3mm (US2–3) needles, cast on 35 sts and work 6 rows in patt as at hem.
Change to 3.75mm (US5) needles and work in St st, inc 1 st at each end of 3rd and every foll 3rd row to 41 sts.
Cont without shaping until sleeve measures 7.5cm/3in.

Shape top

Cast (bind) off 2 sts at beg of next 2 rows. (*37 sts*)
Dec 1 st at each end of every alt row 7 times. (*23 sts*)
Work 4 rows without shaping.
Dec 1 st at each end of the next 6 rows. (*11 sts*)
Cast (bind) off rem 11 sts.

Finishing

Set in sleeves, then sew up side and sleeve seams.
Block or press carefully as given on page 142.
Sew buttons onto button band.
Thread ribbon through eyelets at yoke, on the front of the dress only. Secure with a few stitches.

HAT

Using 3.75mm (US5) needles, cast on 77 sts and work rows 1–6 as for hem of dress.
Cont in St st until work measures 8.5cm/3½in.

Shape top

Row 1: *K9, k2tog; rep from * to end. *(70 sts)*

Row 2 and alt rows: Purl.

Row 3: *K8, k2tog; rep from * to end. *(63 sts)*

Row 5: *K7, k2tog; rep from * to end. *(56 sts)*

Row 7: *K6, k2tog; rep from * to end. *(49 sts)*

Row 9: *K5, k2tog; rep from * to end. *(42 sts)*

Row 11: *K4, k2tog, rep from * to end. *(35 sts)*

Row 13: *K3, k2tog; rep from * to end. *(28 sts)*

Row 14: *P2tog, p2; rep from * to end. *(21 sts)*

Row 15: *K1, k2tog; rep from * to end. *(14 sts)*

Row 16: [P2tog] 7 times.
Break yarn and thread through rem sts, draw up and fasten off.

Finishing

Sew back seam.
Weave in ends.

Optional flower

Using 3.5mm (USE/4) crochet hook, make an adjustable ring around finger. Work [1dc (sc), 1htr (hdc), 2tr (dc), 1htr (hdc), 1dc (sc)] into ring, 4 times. Fasten off. Draw up tail of ring tightly and use to sew flower onto hat.

HEART CHART

KEY

◯	RS: yo
☐	RS: knit / WS: purl
●	RS: purl / WS: knit
╱	RS: k2tog
╲	RS: ssk
⩘	RS: k3tog
☐	repeat
☐	repeat
⋀	sk2po

'Chamomile' Short Christening Dress & Bonnet

SIZE
To fit 0–6 months

FINISHED MEASUREMENTS
Jacket: Chest 48cm/19in **Length (to back neck)** 23cm/9in **Sleeves** 12cm/5in
Bonnet: Crown to brim 14cm/5½in (from picot edge) **Circumference** 33cm/13in
Mittens: Length 13cm/5in (from picot edge) **Circumference** 11cm/4½in

MATERIALS
Yarn Drops Baby Alpaca Silk 4 ply (70% alpaca, 30% silk, 167m/183yd):
3 x 50g/1¾oz balls shade 100 Off White
Needles 1 pair needles size 3.25mm (US3), 1 pair needles size 3.75mm (US5),
one single 3.25mm (US3) needle OR a long stitch holder, 5 stitch holders
Notions 4 buttons, 1cm/⅜in diameter; 2m/2yd ribbon, 1.5cm/⅝in wide

TENSION (GAUGE)
26 sts and 30 rows measure 10cm/4in over St st on 3.75mm (US5) needles
(or size needed to obtain given tension/gauge)

'Snowdrop' Christening Jacket Set

Traditionally, babies wear a long silk or satin dress for a christening, but as churches are often chilly it is useful to have a pretty knitted jacket as an extra layer. This white jacket, bonnet and mittens set is knitted in a luxurious mix of alpaca and silk. With its lace hem and frills, it is decorative enough for any christening, adding a touch of frivolity to a plain gown or dressing up a pair of trousers (pants).

JACKET
Lace pattern
Row 1 (RS): Knit.
Row 2: K1, p1, *yo, p3, sl 1 wyif, p2tog tbl, psso, p3, yo, p1; rep from * 12 times, k1.
Row 3: K1, *k2, yo, k2, sk2po, k2, yo, k1; rep from * 12 times, k2.
Row 4: K1, p1, *p2, yo, p1, sl 1 wyif, p2tog tbl, psso, p1, yo, p3; rep from * 12 times, k1.
Row 5: K1, *k4, yo, sk2po, yo, k3; rep from * 12 times, k2.
Row 6: K1, p1, *p1, k2, p3, k2, p2; rep from * 12 times, k1.
Row 7: K1, *k1, yo, ssk, k1, yo, sk2po, yo, k1, k2tog, yo; rep from * 12 times, k2.
Row 8: K1, p1, *p2, [k1, p3] twice; rep from * 12 times, k1.
Row 9: K1, *k2, yo, ssk, yo, sk2po, yo, k2tog, yo, k1; rep from * 12 times, k2.
Row 10: K1, p1, *p1, k1, p5, k1, p2; rep from * 12 times, k1.
Row 11: K1, *k4, yo, sk2po, yo, k3; rep from * 12 times, k2.
Row 12: K1, p1, *p1, k1, p5, k1, p2; rep from * 12 times, k1.

Frill
Picot edge
Using 3.25mm (US3) needles, cast on 123 sts and work 4 rows St st, beg with a purl row.

Row 5 (WS): P2, *yf, p2tog; rep from * to end, p1.

Beg with a knit row, work 3 rows St st.

Row 9: Purl next row picking up 1 st from cast-on edge and purling it tog with st on needle to form picot hem.

Change to 3.75mm (US5) needles and work rows 1–5 of lace patt.

Row 6: Purl. **

Row 7: K1, *k2, k2tog; rep from * to last 2 sts, k2. (93 sts)

Break yarn and leave these 93 sts on the needle or transfer them onto a stitch holder.

Body
(Worked in one piece to armholes.)
Using 3.25mm (US3) needles, cast on 123 sts.

Work 9 rows as for picot edge of frill.

Change to 3.75mm (US5) needles and work 2 reps of lace patt, then rows 1–5 again.

Cont in St st until work measures 14cm/5½in, ending with a WS row.

Split for fronts and back
Right front
Row 1: K25, turn.

Row 2: Purl to end.

Row 3: K to last 3 sts, k2tog, k1. (24 sts)

Row 4: As row 2.

Row 5: As row 3. (23 sts)

Row 6: P4, *p2tog, p1; rep from * to last 4 sts, p4. (18 sts)

Break yarn and leave sts on a holder.

Back
With RS facing, rejoin yarn to back.
Cast (bind) off 6 sts, k60, turn. (61 sts)

Row 1: Purl to end.

Row 2: K1, ssk, k to last 3 sts, k2tog, k1. (59 sts)

Row 3: As row 1.

Row 4: As row 2. (57 sts)

Row 5: P5, *p2tog, p1; rep from * to last 4 sts, p4. (41 sts)

Break yarn and leave sts on a holder.

Left front
With RS facing, rejoin yarn to left front. Cast (bind) off 6 sts, k to end. (25 sts)

Row 1: Purl.

Row 2: K1, ssk, k to end. (24 sts)

Row 3: As row 1.

Row 4: As row 2. (23 sts)

Row 5: P4, *p1, p2tog; rep from * to last 4 sts, p4. (18 sts)

Break yarn and leave sts on a holder.

Sleeves (make 2)
Using 3.25mm (US3) needles, cast on 32 sts and work picot edge as for frill, beg with p1.

Change to 3.75mm (US5) needles and cont in St st, inc 1 st (kfb) at each end of 5th and every foll 4th row to 42 sts.

Cont without shaping until sleeve measures 12.5cm/5in.

Shape top
Cast (bind) off 3 sts at beg next 2 rows. (36 sts)

Row 1: K1, ssk, k to last 3 sts, k2tog, k1. (34 sts)

Row 2: Purl.

Row 3: As row 1. (32 sts)

Row 4: As row 2.

Row 5: As row 1. (30 sts)

Break yarn and leave sts on a holder.

Yoke
Using size 3.75mm (US5) needles and with RS facing:
Knit across sts of right front (18 sts), first sleeve (30 sts), back (41 sts),

second sleeve (30 sts) and left front (18 sts). (137 sts)

Rows 1–3: Work 3 rows St st, beg with a purl row.

Row 4: *K3, k2tog; rep from * to last 2 sts, k2. (110 sts)

Rows 5–8: Work 4 rows St st.

Row 9: P6, *p2tog, p4; rep from * to last 2 sts, p2. (93 sts)

Row 10 (RS): Place sts from frill in front of sts of yoke and knit through both sets of sts tog across the row.

Rows 11–13: Work 3 rows St st.

Row 14: K8, *k2tog, k3; rep from * to last 5 sts, k5. (77 sts)

Rows 15–17: Work 3 rows St st.

Row 18: K2tog, [k2, k2tog] 18 times to last 3 sts, k1, k2tog. (57 sts)

Rows 19–21: Work 3 rows St st. Change to 3.25mm (US3) needles and work 8 rows as for picot hem.
Cast (bind) off.
Fold picot hem in half and stitch to inside of neck.

Button band
Using 3.25mm (US3) needles, starting at top of picot edge, pick up and knit 61 sts along left front (approx 3 sts for every 4 rows).
Work 8 rows garter st (knit every row).
Cast (bind) off.

Buttonhole band
Starting at bottom of picot hem of right front, work 4 rows as for button band.

Next row (WS): K3, *yf, k2tog, k5; rep from * 3 times more, k to end.
Work 3 rows garter st.
Cast (bind) off.

Finishing
Weave in ends.
Block or press carefully as given on page 142.

Stitch raglan seams together. Sew up sleeve seams. Sew on buttons.

BONNET
Frill
Using 3.25mm (US3) needles, cast on 103 sts and work as for jacket frill (including picot edge) to **.

Row 7 (dec row): [K3, k2tog] to last 3 sts, k3. *(83 sts)*
Break off yarn and leave sts on needle or a stitch holder.

Main section
Using 3.25mm (US3) needles, cast on 83 sts and work 4 rows [K1, p1] rib. Change to 3.75mm (US5) needles and work 10 rows St st, beg with a k row.
Next row: Place frill on top of piece and holding the 2 needles together, knit each st together with corresponding stitch from frill, across the row.
Cont in St st until work measures 11cm/4½in from picot edge, ending with a RS row.
Next row (WS): P2tog, p to last 2 sts, p2tog. *(81 sts)*

Shape crown
Row 1: *K7, k2tog; rep from * to end. *(72 sts)*
Row 2 and alt rows: Knit.
Row 3: *K6, k2tog; rep from * to end. *(63 sts)*
Row 5: *K5, k2tog; rep from * to end. *(54 sts)*
Row 7: *K4, k2tog; rep from * to end. *(45 sts)*
Cont dec on alt rows with one stitch less between dec each time until 18 sts rem.
Next row: K2tog to end. *(9 sts)*
Break yarn, thread yarn through rem 9 sts, draw up and fasten off.

Join back seam, starting at crown and finishing 2.5cm/1in beyond crown.

Using 3.25mm (US3) needles, pick up and knit 50 sts along bottom edge, working through both layers of frill and bonnet. Work 4 rows [k1, p1] rib. Cast (bind) off.

Finishing
Sew ribbons to front edge.

MITTENS (MAKE 2)
Using 3.25mm (US3) needles, cast on 30 sts and work picot edge as for frill, beg with p1.
Work 4 rows St st beg with a knit row.
Next row (RS, eyelet row): K2, [yo, k2tog, k1] to last st, k1.
Work 18 rows St st.

Shape top
Row 1: [K1, ssk, k9, k2tog, k1] twice. *(26 sts)*
Rows 2 and 4: Purl.
Row 3: [K1, ssk, k7, k2tog, k1] twice. *(22 sts)*
Row 5: [K1, ssk, k5, k2tog, k1] twice. *(18 sts)*
Cast (bind) off.

Finishing
Fold mittens in half and join side seam. Thread ribbon through eyelet holes.

JACKET CHART

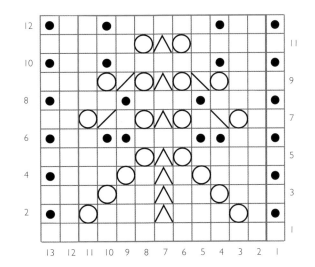

KEY

☐	RS: knit / WS: purl
◯	RS: yo / WS: yo
◸	RS: ssk / WS: p2tog tbl
△	RS: sk2po / WS: sl 1 wyif, p2tog, tbl, psso
◿	RS: k2tog / WS: p2tog
●	RS: purl / WS: knit
☐	repeat

'Snowdrop' Christening Jacket Set

FINISHED MEASUREMENTS
Shawl 81 [130]cm/32 [51]in square

MATERIALS
Yarn Jamieson's Ultra (50% Shetland wool, 50% lambswool, 195m/213yd):
8 [19] x 25g/1oz balls shade 104 Natural White
Needles 1 pair needles size 5mm (US8)

TENSION (GAUGE)
19 sts and 34 rows measure 10cm/4in over garter st on 5mm (US8) needles
(although tension/gauge is not vital for this item)

'Heather' Lace-Edged Shawl

Known as a head shawl, this small shawl would have been used to keep the baby warm when coming home from the hospital. Unlike more decorative christening shawls, which were intended for display as well as warmth, head shawls are usually fairly plain. This one has a garter-stitch centre and a border of Old Shale stitch. It is knitted in a 2-ply wool from the sheep native to the Shetland Islands, in the traditional undyed natural white.

SHAWL
Centre section
Cast on 86 [158] sts.
Work in garter st (knit every row) until work measures 46 [85]cm/ 18 [33]in.

First border
Work the lace border in four sections as follows:
Row 1 (RS): K4, *[yo, k1] 6 times, [k2tog] 6 times; rep from * to last 10 sts, [yo, k1] 6 times, k4. *(92 [164] sts)*
Work 3 rows in garter st.
Row 5: K4, yo, k1, k2tog, *[yo, k1] 6 times, [k2tog] 6 times; rep from * to last 13 sts, [yo, k1] 6 times, k2tog, yo, k1, k4. *(98 [170] sts)*
Work 3 rows in garter st.
Row 9: K4, [yo, k1] twice, [k2tog] twice, *[yo, k1] 6 times, [k2tog] 6 times; rep from * to last 16 sts, [yo, k1] 6 times, [k2tog] twice, [yo, k1] twice, k4. *(104 [176] sts)*
Work 3 rows in garter st.
Row 13: K4, [yo, k1] 3 times, [k2tog] 3 times, *[yo, k1] 6 times, [k2tog] 6 times; rep from * to last 19 sts, [yo, k1] 6 times, [k2tog] 3 times, [yo, k1] 3 times, k4. *(110 [182] sts)*
Work 3 rows in garter st.
Row 17: K4, [yo, k1] 4 times, [k2tog] 4 times *[yo, k1] 6 times, [k2tog] 6 times; rep from * to last 22 sts, [yo, k1] 6 times, [k2tog] 4 times, [yo, k1] 4 times, k4. *(116 [188] sts)*
Work 3 rows in garter st.
Row 21: K4, [yo, k1] 5 times, [k2tog] 5 times, *[yo, k1] 6 times, [k2tog] 6 times; rep from * to last 25 sts, [yo, k1] 6 times, [k2tog] 5 times, [yo, k1] 5 times, k4. *(122 [194] sts)*

Work 3 rows in garter st.
Rep these 24 rows once [twice] more. *(158 [266] sts)*
Next row: Knit.
Cast (bind) off loosely.

Second border
With RS of work facing, pick up and knit 86 [158] sts along the cast-on edge.
Knit 1 row, then work as for first border.

Work borders on the other two sides in the same way.

Finishing
Join the corners with loosely worked herringbone stitch.
Pin out points of lace to measurements and block as given on page 142.

SIZE
To fit 3–6 [6–12] months

FINISHED MEASUREMENTS
Vest: Chest 46 [50]cm/18 [20]in **Length (to back neck)** 28 [32]cm/11 [12½]in
Shorts: Length 28 [31]cm/11 [12]in

MATERIALS
Yarn Sirdar Snuggly 4 ply (55% nylon, 45% acrylic, 226m/247yd):
2 [3] x 50g/1¾oz balls shade 251 White
Needles 1 pair needles size 3.75mm (US5), 1 pair needles size 3mm (US2–3),
1 stitch holder, 1 cable needle
Notions 2 buttons, 1cm/⅜in diameter; 1m/1yd narrow elastic,
approx 4mm/¼in wide

TENSION (GAUGE)
27 sts and 30 rows measure 10cm/4in over St st on 3.75mm (US5) needles (or size
needed to obtain given tension/gauge)

'Wood Sorrel' Christening Vest & Shorts

Christening gowns evolved in the eighteenth century, when babies no longer wore
swaddling clothes. Babies of either sex would wear a long dress, which had often
been handed down through the family. Fashions change, and these days many
mothers prefer to put their baby boy in trousers (pants). I haven't found any
vintage patterns for this style, so I designed this outfit for a more contemporary
look. The knitted vest has a pretty lace pattern alongside a more boyish cable
stitch. It is smart enough for a christening or, in a colour, for any other occasion.

VEST
Back
Using 3mm (US2–3) needles, cast on 62
[68] sts and work 4cm/1½in [k1, p1] rib.
Change to 3.75mm (US5) needles
and work in St st until work measures
16 [19]cm/6½ [7½]in.

Shape armhole
Cont in St st, cast (bind) off 3 sts at
beg of next 2 rows. (56 [62] sts)
Dec 1 st at each end of next 2 rows,
then at each end of next and foll 3 alt
rows. (44 [50] sts)
Cont until work measures 10.5 [12]cm/

4¼ [4¾]in from beg of armhole shaping,
ending with a WS row.

Shape shoulder
Cast (bind) off 6 sts at beg of next 2 rows,
and 5 sts at beg foll 2 rows. (22 [28] sts)
Break yarn and leave rem sts on a holder.

Front

Using 3mm (US2–3) needles, cast on 62 [68] sts and work 4cm/1½in [k1, p1] rib. Change to 3.75mm (US5) needles and work in patt as follows:

Row 1: K10 [13], *p2, k3, p2, k4, p2, k3, p2*, k6, rep from * to * k10 [13].

Row 2: P10 [13], *k2, p3, k2, p4, k2, p3, k2*, p6, rep from * to *, p10 [13].

Row 3: K10 [13], *p2, k1, yo, k2tog, p2, k4, p2, k1, yo, k2tog, p2*, k6, rep from * to *, k10 [13].

Row 4: P10 [13], *k2, p3, k2, p4, k2, p3, k2*, p6, rep from * to *, p10 [13].

Row 5: K10 [13], *p2, k3, p2, 2/2 FC, p2, k3, p2*, k6, rep from * to *, k10 [13].

Row 6: P10 [13], *k2, p3, k2, p4, k2, p3, k2*, p6, rep from * to *, p10 [13].

Rep these 6 rows until work measures same as back to armholes, ending with a WS row.

Shape armholes and neck

Row 1 (RS): Cast (bind) off 3 sts, patt 28 [31] sts, turn.

Cont to work on these 28 [31] sts.

Row 2: K1, p2tog, patt to last 3 sts, p2togtbl, k1. (26 [29] sts)

Row 3: K1, ssk, patt to end. (25 [28] sts)

Row 4: K1, patt to end.

Cont dec 1 st at armhole edge of next and foll 3 alt rows and AT THE SAME TIME dec 1 st at neck edge on next and every 3rd row until 11 sts rem. Cont to same length as back, ending with a WS row.

Shoulder

Next row: Cast (bind) off 6 sts at beg of next row, and 5 sts at beg of foll alt row.

Rejoin yarn to RS and work other half of neck to match.

Neckband

Join right shoulder seam.

Using 3mm (US2–3) needles, pick up and knit 29 [33] sts down left side of neck, pick up horizontal bar between centre sts and knit into back of it, pick up and knit 29 [33] sts up right side of neck, and k22 [28] from back neck holder. (81 [95] sts)

Work 5 rows [k1, p1] rib, dec 1 st at each side of centre st on every row. Cast (bind) off in rib, still dec each side of centre st.

Left shoulder

With RS facing and using 3mm (US2–3) needles, pick up and knit 11 sts from front shoulder and 6 sts from edge of neckband.

Rib 2 rows.

Next row (WS, buttonhole row): Rib 4, yo, k2tog, rib 5, yo k2tog, rib to end.

Work 2 more rows rib.

Cast (bind) off.

Work back shoulder to match, omitting buttonholes.

Armbands

With RS facing, using 3mm (US2–3) needles and starting at the underarm, pick up and knit 61 [69] sts around armhole edge, working through both layers of button and buttonhole flap on left arm.
Work 5 rows [k1, p1] rib.
Cast (bind) off.

Finishing

Join side seams.
Sew buttons to left shoulder.
Weave in ends.
Block or press carefully as given on page 142.

SHORTS
Front

Using 3mm (US2–3) needles, cast on 62 [68] sts and work 3cm/1¼in [k1, p1] rib.
Change to 3.75mm (US5) needles and work 18 [20]cm/7 [8]in St st.

Shape legs and crotch

Row 1: K30 [33], kfb in next 2 sts, k30 [33]. (64 [70] sts)
Row 2: Purl.
Row 3: K30 [33], kfb in next st, k2, inc in next st, k30 [33]. (66 [72] sts)
Row 4: Purl.
Cont inc on alt rows in this way until there are 72 [78] sts, ending on a WS row.
Next row: K30 [33], turn and leave rem sts on a holder.
Work 5cm/2in St st on these 30 [33] sts.

Change to 3mm (US2–3) needles and work 5 rows [k1, p1] rib.
Cast (bind) off.

Leaving 12 centre sts on the holder, rejoin yarn with RS facing and work other leg to match.

Back

Using 3mm (US2–3) needles, cast on 62 [68] sts and work 3cm/1¼in in [k1, p1] rib.
Change to 3.75mm (US5) needles and work 2 rows St st.

Shape back

Next row (RS): K54 [60], turn.
Next row: P46 [52], turn.
Next row: K38 [44], turn.
Next row: P30 [36], turn.
Next row: K22 [28], turn.
Next row: P14 [20], turn.
Next row: Knit to end.
Next row: Purl to end.
Cont in St st without shaping until work measures same as front to crotch.
Shape legs and crotch as for front.

Finishing

Join sts at crotch by grafting or with a 3-needle cast-off (bind-off) (on the inside).
Join leg seams and side seams.
Weave in all ends.
Thread elastic through centre row of rib, weaving it under the knit sts.
Block or press carefully as given on page 142.

VEST CABLE AND LACE CHART

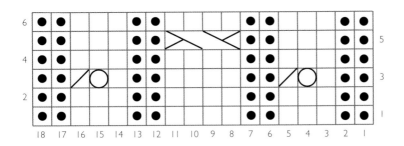

KEY

☐ RS: knit
WS: purl

╱ RS: k2tog

● RS: purl
WS: knit

◯ RS: yo

⧖ RS: 2/2 FC

'Out & About'

Lacy jacket, bootees and bonnet sets

The first pram (buggy) was a wicker basket on wheels, invented by the architect William Kent in 1733 for the Duke of Devonshire's children. By the 1920s the pram, or baby-carriage, was familiar throughout Britain. It was thought that babies should have an 'airing' every day for the sake of their health. As the baby's lower half was hidden by the pram cover, outdoor wear was just for the upper half. Patterns for matinée sets – jacket, bonnet, mittens and sometimes bootees – were numerous. The designs included in this chapter are typical of the era, and each one has some sort of decorative feature in the form of lace stitches. Matinée sets often had the added trim of ribbons and bows, and were worn by both boys and girls; the only concession to gender was that boys were usually dressed in blue and girls in pink.

SIZE
To fit 0–6 [6–9] months
To fit chest 41 [46]cm/16 [18]in

FINISHED MEASUREMENTS
Jacket: Chest 48 [53]cm/19 [21]in **Length (to back neck)** 23 [25]cm/9 [10]in
Sleeves 13 [15]cm/5 [6]in
Bonnet: Crown to brim 12cm/4¾in **Circumference** 32cm/12½in
Bootees: Foot length 11cm/4½in **Circumference** 13cm/5¼in

MATERIALS
Yarn DMC Natura Just Cotton 4 ply (100% cotton, 155m/170yd): 3 [4] x 50g/1¾oz balls shade Spring Rose
Needles 1 pair needles size 2.75mm (US2), 1 pair needles size 3.75mm (US5), 4 stitch holders
Notions 4 buttons, 1cm/⅜in diameter; 1m/1yd ribbon, 2cm/¾in wide; 50cm/20in ribbon, 1cm/⅜in wide

TENSION (GAUGE)
24 sts and 30 rows measure 10cm/4in over lace pattern on 3.75mm (US5) needles
(or size needed to obtain given tension/gauge)

'Sweet Violet' Lacy Matinée Set

Matinée sets came about as a result of the pram (buggy), which grew in popularity during the Victorian era. Because only the top half of the baby could be seen, these jacket and hat sets gradually replaced carrying shawls, and what at first was simply a means of keeping the top half warm later turned into something more elaborate. As handmade needle lace was costly, the amount used in a garment indicated the status of the owner; knitted lace was a less expensive way of continuing this custom.

JACKET
Lace pattern
Row 1: K5, *k2, k2tog, yo, k3; rep from * to last 5 sts, k5.
Row 2: K4, p1, *p1, p2tog tbl, yo, p1, yo, p2tog, p1; rep from * to last 5 sts, p1, k4.

Row 3: K5, *k2tog, yo, k3, yo, ssk; rep from * to last 5 sts, k5.
Row 4: K4, p to last 4, k4.
Row 5: K5, *yo, ssk, k5; rep from * to last 5 sts, k5.
Row 6: K4, p1, * yo, p2tog, p2, p2tog tbl, yo, p1; rep from * to last 5 sts, p1, k4.

Row 7: K5, *k2, yo, ssk, k2tog, yo, k1; rep from * to last 5 sts, k5.
Row 8: K4, p to last 4, k4.

Sleeves (make 2)
Using 2.75mm (US2) needles, cast on 30 sts and knit 4 rows.

Row 1 (inc row):

First size: K1, [kfb in next st, k1] to last 3 sts, kfb in next st, k2. *(44 sts)*

Second size: K2, [kfb in next st] to end. *(58 sts)*

Row 2: Knit.

First size only:

Row 3: K6, [kfb in next st, k4] to last 3sts, k3. *(51 sts)*

Both sizes:

Change to 3.75mm (US5) needles. Cont in lace patt from row 1, but with a k1 at beg and end of each row instead of k5.

When work measures 13 [15]cm/ 5 [6]in, and ending on a row 4 or 8, break off yarn and leave sts on a holder.

Body

(Worked in one piece to armholes.) Using 2.75mm (US2) needles, cast on 164 [192] sts and k4 rows.

Change to 3.75mm (US5) needles and work in lace patt for approx 14 [16]cm/ 5½ [6½]in ending after a patt row 1.

Divide for fronts and back
Left front

Row 2 (WS): K4, p1, *p1, p2tog tbl, yo, p1, yo, p2tog, p1; rep from * 5 [6] times. Turn, and work on these 40 [47] sts.

Row 3 (RS): *K2tog, yo, k3, yo, ssk; rep from * to last 5 sts, k5.

Row 4: K4, p to end.

Row 5: K7, *yo, ssk, k5; rep from * to last 5 sts, k5.

Row 6: K4, p1, * yo, p2tog, p2, p2tog tbl, yo, p1; rep from * to end.

Row 7: *K2, yo, ssk, k2tog, yo, k1; rep from * to last 5 sts, k5.

Row 8: K4, p to end.

Break off yarn and leave sts on a holder.

Back

Rejoin yarn to WS and work in patt from row 2 as for left front, from * 12 [14] times, omitting the garter sts at each end. *(84 [98] sts)*

Break off yarn and leave sts on a holder.

Right front

Rejoin yarn to WS and cont in patt as follows:

Row 2 (WS): *P1, p2tog tbl, yo, p1, yo, p2tog, p1; rep from * 5 [6] times, p1, k4. *(40 [47] sts)*

Row 3 (RS): K5, *k2tog, yo, k3, yo, ssk; rep from * to end.

Row 4: P to last 4 sts, k4.

Row 5: K5, *yo, ssk, k5; rep from * to end.

Row 6: P4, p2tog tbl, yo, p1, * yo, p2tog, p2, p2tog tbl, yo, p1; rep from * to last 5 sts, p1, k4.

Row 7: K5, *k2, yo, ssk, k2tog, yo, k1; rep from * to end.

Row 8: P to last 4 sts, k4.

Do not break off yarn but cont for yoke.

Yoke

Using 2.75mm (US2) needles and with RS facing, knit across all sts in the foll order; right front, sleeve, back, sleeve, left front. *(266 [308] sts)*
Knit 1 row.

Dec for yoke first size

Row 1 (RS): K4, [k2tog, k1] 33 times, [k2tog] 30 times, [k2tog, k1] 33 times, k4. *(170 sts)*
Row 2: Knit.
Row 3 (buttonhole row): K2, yo, k2tog, k to end.
Rows 4 and 5: Knit.
Row 6: K4, [k2tog, k11] 5 times, k2tog, k28, [k2tog, k11] 5 times, k2tog, k4. *(158 sts)*
Rows 7 and 8: Knit.
Row 9: K4, [k2tog, k10] 5 times, k2tog, k26, [k2tog, k10] 5 times, k2tog, k4. *(146 sts)*
Row 10: Knit.
Row 11 (buttonhole row): K2, yf, k2tog, k to end.
Row 12: K4, [k2tog, k9] 5 times, k2tog, k24, [k2tog, k9] 5 times, k2tog, k4. *(134 sts)*
Cont dec in this way on every 3rd row, and making buttonholes at beg of every 8th row until there are 74 sts. (The last dec row [27th] will also be a buttonhole row.)
Knit 2 rows.
Cast (bind) off.

Dec for yoke 2nd size

Row 1 (RS): K4, [k2tog, k1] 34 times, [k2tog] 48 times, [k2tog, k1] 34 times, k4. *(192 sts)*
Rows 2 and 3: Knit.
Row 4: K4, [k2tog, k13] 5 times, k2tog, k30, [k2tog, k13] 5 times, k2tog, k4. *(180 sts)*
Rows 5 and 6: Knit.
Row 7 (buttonhole row): K2, yo,

k2tog, [k2tog, k12] 5 times, k2tog, k28, [k2tog, k12] 5 times, k2tog, k4. *(168 sts)*
Rows 8 and 9: Knit.
Cont dec in this way on every 3rd row until 72 sts rem, making buttonholes on every 8th row. (The last dec row [31st] will also be a buttonhole row.)
Knit 2 rows.
Cast (bind) off.

Finishing

Sew up side and sleeve seams.
Sew buttons onto button band.
Block or press carefully as given on page 142.

BONNET

Using 2.75mm (US2) needles, cast on 72 sts and work 5cm/2in in garter st (knit every row).
Change to 3.75mm (US5) needles and work 20 rows in lace patt, working the first and last st as k1.

Shape back

Row 1: K46, k2tog, turn.
Row 2: K21, p2tog, turn.
Rep last row until all side sts are worked off. *(22 sts)*
Break off yarn and leave sts on a holder.
Fold garter-st band in half towards the RS.
Using 2.75mm (US2) needles and beg at front of fold with RS facing, pick up and knit 24 sts evenly along lace edge, [k2tog, k4, k2tog, k6, k2tog, k4, k2tog] from holder, pick up and knit 24 sts along other lace edge to front of fold.
Knit 4 rows.
Cast (bind) off.

Finishing

Weave in all ends.
Block or press carefully as given on page 142.

Sew 2cm/¾in wide ribbon to front edges.

BOOTEES (MAKE 2)

Using 2.75mm (US2) needles, cast on 37 sts and knit 4 rows.
Change to 3.75mm (US5) needles and work 12 rows in lace patt as for sleeves of jacket (k1 at each end).
Next row: Knit.
Next row: Purl.
Next row (eyelets row): K1, [yo, k2tog, k1] to end.
Next row: Purl.
Next row: Knit.

Shape foot

Cont in garter st.
Next row: K25, turn.
Next row: K13, turn.
Cont on these 13 sts in garter st for 17 more rows then pick up and knit 17 sts along side of instep.
Knit 12 sts to end of row.
Next row: K42, pick up and knit 17 sts along other side of instep, knit 12 rem sts. *(71 sts)*
Work 10 rows garter st.

Shape sole

Row 1: K2tog, k31, k2tog, k1, k2tog, k to last 2 sts, k2tog.
Rows 2 and 4: Knit.
Row 3: K2tog, k29, k2tog, k1, k2tog, k to last 2 sts, k2tog.
Row 5: K2tog, k27, k2tog, k1, k2tog, k to last 2 sts, k2tog.
Cast (bind) off.

Finishing

Join side and sole seams.
Thread 1cm/⅜in ribbon through eyelets.

SIZE
To fit 0–6 months

FINISHED MEASUREMENTS
Jacket: Chest 51cm/20in **Length (to back neck)** 25cm/10in
Sleeves 12cm/4¾in
Beanie: Crown to brim 12.5cm/5in **Circumference** 31.5cm/12in
Bootees: Foot length 10cm/4in **Circumference** 17cm/6½in

MATERIALS
Yarn Artesano Definition Sock Yarn (75% wool, 25% polyamide, 400m/437yd):
2 x 100g/3½oz balls shade Mushy Peas
Needles 1 pair needles size 3mm (US2–3), 1 40cm/16in circular needle or dpns
size 3mm (US2–3), 4 stitch holders
Notions 4 buttons, 1cm/⅜in diameter; 75cm/30in ribbon, 1.5cm/½in wide

TENSION (GAUGE)
27 sts and 44 rows measure 10cm/4in over ridge pattern on 3mm (US2–3) needles
(or size needed to obtain given tension/gauge)

'Buttercup' Scalloped-Edge Matinée Set

It was always thought important to keep a baby's head and feet warm, so most matinée jackets came with a matching hat and bootees; this one, dating from the 1940s, is no exception. The traditional Old Shale stitch pattern continues the custom of dressing a baby in lace. I have never found a pattern for a plain matinée set from later than the 1930s. Before this the jackets were often made from quilted fabric, with matching padded hats to protect the baby's head if it fell. This set offers no protection from bumps but it makes a very pretty layer of extra warmth.

Jacket ridge pattern
Row 1: Knit.
Row 2: Purl.
Row 3: Knit.
Row 4: Purl.
Row 5: Knit.

Row 6: Knit.

Beanie ridge pattern
(Worked in the round.)
Round 1: Purl.
Rounds 2–6: Knit.

**Jacket and bootees
Old Shale pattern**
Row 1: [K2tog] 4 times, *[yo, k1] 8 times, [k2tog] 8 times; rep from * to last 16 sts, [yo, k1] 8 times, [k2tog] 4 times.

Row 2: Purl.
Row 3: Knit.
Row 4: Purl.

Beanie Old Shale pattern
(Worked in the round.)
Round 1: [K2tog] 4 times, *[yo, k1]
8 times, [k2tog] 8 times; rep from *
to last 16 sts, [yo, k1] 8 times, [k2tog]
4 times.
Rounds 2–4: Knit.

JACKET
(Worked from the top down.)

Neckband
Using 3mm (US2–3) needles, cast on
82 sts.
Knit 6 rows.

Yoke and raglan
Row 1 (RS): K16, yo, k1, yo, k10, yo,
k1, yo, k26, yo, k1, yo, k10, yo, k1, yo,
k16. (90 sts)
Row 2: Purl.
Row 3: K17, yo, k1, yo, k12, yo, k1,
yo, k28, yo, k1, yo, k12, yo, k1, yo, k17.
(98 sts)
Row 4: Purl.
Cont inc in this way on every alt row
and working ridge patt for jacket until
there are 226 sts (18 rows of eyelets).
End with a row 6 of ridge patt and
break off yarn.

Divide work for body and sleeves
With RS facing, place 34 sts of left front
on a stitch holder, rejoin yarn and knit
48 sts of sleeve.
Place 62 sts of back onto stitch holder,
place 48 sts of right sleeve onto stitch
holder, and place 34 sts of right front
onto stitch holder.

Return to sts of left sleeve.
Next row (inc row): Cast on 4 sts at

beg of row. P5, *pfb in next st, p2; rep
from * 15 times to last 2 sts, pfb, p1,
cast on 4 sts at end of row. (72 sts)
Work sleeve in Old Shale patt for
11cm/4½in ending after a row 1.
Work 4 rows garter st (knit every row).
Cast (bind) off.

Return to sts for 2nd sleeve and work
to match.

Body
With RS facing, knit 34 sts of left front
from holder, pick up and knit 8 sts from
those cast on at underarm, knit across
62 sts of back, pick up and knit 8 sts
from underarm of right sleeve, knit
across 34 sts of right front. (146 sts)
Inc row (WS): P5, *pfb in next st, p2;
rep from * to last 3 sts, p3. (192 sts)
Work in Old Shale patt to 14cm/5½in,
ending after a row 1.
Work 4 rows garter st.
Cast (bind) off.

Front edgings
With RS facing and starting at bottom
edge, pick up and knit 68 sts (approx
4 sts for every 5 rows) along right
front edge.
Knit 2 rows.
Next row (buttonhole row):
K3, *yo, k2tog, k6; rep from * 4 times,
knit to end.
Knit 2 rows.
Cast (bind) off.

Work left front edging to match,
omitting buttonholes.

Finishing
Join underarm sleeve seams.
Weave in ends.
Sew on buttons.
Block or press carefully as given on
page 142.

BEANIE
(Worked in the round.)
Using a 3mm (US2–3) circular needle
or dpns, cast on 96 sts and work 5
rnds garter st (knit 1 rnd, purl 1 rnd).
Work Old Shale patt for beanie
4 times, then rnds 1 and 2 again.
Change to ridge patt for beanie
and work to 9cm/3½in, ending
after a purl rnd.

Dec for crown
Round 1: Knit.
Round 2: *K10, k2tog; rep from * to
end. (88 sts)
Round 3: Knit.
Round 4: *K9, k2tog; rep from * to
end. (80 sts)
Round 5: Knit.
Round 6: *P8, p2tog; rep from * to
end. (72 sts)
Cont dec on alt rnds working in ridge
patt until the rnd [k4, k2tog] has been
worked. (40 sts)
Cont to dec on every rnd until 8 sts rem.
Break off yarn, leaving a tail of approx
12cm/5in. Thread yarn through the
rem sts, draw up tightly and fasten off.

Finishing
Weave in ends.
Block or press carefully as given on
page 142.

BOOTEES (MAKE 2)
Using 3mm (US2–3) needles, cast on
48 sts and work 5 rows garter st (knit
every row).
Cont in Old Shale patt as for jacket for
7cm/3in, ending with a RS row.
Next row (dec row, WS): P16,
*p2tog, p2; rep from * 3 times more,
p16. (44 sts)
Next row (eyelet row): K1, [yo,
k2tog] to end, k1.
Next row: Purl.

Instep

Next row: K28, leave rem 16 sts on a holder, and turn.

Next row: P12, leave rem 16 sts on a holder, and turn.

Work in ridge patt as for jacket on these 12 sts for 24 rows.

Break off yarn and leave sts on a holder.

Next row (RS): K16 from first holder, pick up and knit 12 sts along side of instep, k12 from holder, pick up and knit 12 sts along other side of instep, k16 from holder. *(68 sts)*

Sole

Work 5 rows St st, beg with a purl row.

Row 6: K2tog, k24, k2tog, k12, k2tog, k24, k2tog. *(64 sts)*

Rows 7, 9 and 11: Purl.

Row 8: K2tog, k22, k2tog, k12, k2tog, k22, k2tog. *(60 sts)*

Row 10: K2tog, k20, k2tog, k12, k2tog, k20, k2tog. *(56 sts)*

Cast (bind) off.

Finishing

Sew sole and back seam.

Weave in ends.

Block or press carefully as given on page 142.

Thread ribbon through eyelets and tie in a bow.

SIZE
To fit 0–6 months

FINISHED MEASUREMENTS
Jacket: Actual chest size 44cm/17½in
Length (to back neck) 25cm/10in **Sleeves** 17cm/6½in
Bonnet: Crown to brim 16.5cm/6½in **Circumference** 28cm/11in
Bootees: Foot length 10cm/4in **Circumference** 14cm/5½in

MATERIALS
Yarn Sublime Baby Cashmere Merino Silk DK (75% extra fine merino wool, 20% silk, 5% cashmere, 116m/127yd): 4 x 50g/1¾oz balls shade 276 Skipper
Needles 1 pair needles size 3.75mm (US5), plus an additional single needle for 3-needle cast-off (bind-off), 1 pair needles size 3.25mm (US3), 2 stitch holders, 3 safety pins or stitch markers for marking sleeves
Notions 1 button, 1.5cm/⅝in diameter; 2m/2yd ribbon, 1cm/⅜in wide

TENSION (GAUGE)
23 sts and 30 rows measure 10cm/4in over St st on 3.75mm (US5) needles
(or size needed to obtain given tension/gauge)

'Bryony' Eyelet-Stitch Matinée Set

This less elaborate matinée set, but still with a little touch of lace, is ideal for a new knitter to make because there is very little shaping. The jacket back and fronts are simple rectangles and the sleeves are picked up along the armhole edge and knitted downwards, so you can make them as long as you want. The ribbon trim at the cuffs gives the jacket an extra decorative touch. It is knitted here in a luxury yarn, but any double-knitting (worsted) weight could be used for equally pretty results.

JACKET
Eyelet pattern
Row 1: Knit.
Row 2: Purl.
Row 3: Knit.
Row 4: Purl.
Row 5: Knit.
Row 6: Purl.
Row 7: Knit.
Row 8: Knit.
Row 9: Knit.
Row 10: K1, *k2tog, yo; rep from * to last st, k1.
Row 11: Knit.
Row 12: Knit.
These 12 rows form the patt.

Back

Using 3.75mm (US5) needles, cast on 52 sts and knit 6 rows. Work in eyelet patt for 15cm/6in. Mark each end of last row, for position of sleeves, with a removable marker or safety pin. Cont in patt for another 10cm/4in.

Break yarn and leave sts on a holder.

Right front

Cast on 28 sts and, keeping the first 4 sts at front edge in garter st throughout, work as back until front measures 23cm/9in, ending with a WS row.

Shape neck
Next row (RS): Cast (bind) off 8 sts at neck edge, patt to end. *(20 sts)*
Dec 1 st at same edge of next 4 rows. *(16 sts)*

Cont in patt without further shaping until work measures same as back. Break yarn and leave sts on a holder.

Work left front to match, reversing shaping and position of front edge, ending with a WS row.
Do not break yarn.

Shoulders

Slip 16 sts from the back left shoulder onto a needle, and holding it (WS together) alongside the needle with sts from the left front, use a third needle to cast (bind) off both sets of sts together (3-needle cast-off/bind-off). This will seam the shoulders on the outside of the jacket.
Do the same for the right shoulder, leaving the rem 20 sts on a holder for the back neck.

Neckband

Using 3.25mm (US3) needles and with RS facing, pick up and knit 8 sts from cast-off (bound-off) edge of right front neck and 8 sts along neck edge, knit 20 sts from back holder, pick up and knit 8 sts along left neck edge and 8 sts from cast-off (bound-off) sts on left front neck. (52 sts)
Knit 2 rows.
Next row (WS): K2, *yo, k2tog; rep from * to end.
Knit 2 rows.
Cast (bind) off.

Sleeves (make 2)

Using 3.75mm (US5) needles, pick up and knit 54 sts between markers (approx 1 st every row).
Work in eyelet patt for 15cm/6in.
Knit 6 rows garter st.
Cast (bind) off.

Finishing

Set in sleeves, then sew up side and sleeve seams.
Sew button at neck edge.
Block or press carefully as given on page 142.
Thread ribbon through eyelets on cuffs and tie in a bow (optional).

BONNET

Using 3.75mm (US5) needles, cast on 63 sts and knit 6 rows.
Keeping 5 sts at beg and end in garter st, work eyelet patt as for jacket 3 times.
Dec 1 st at beg and end of last row 12.
(61 sts)

Shape crown

Row 1: *K8, k2tog; rep from * to last st, k1. (55 sts)
Row 2 and alt rows: Purl.
Row 3: *K7, k2tog; rep from * to last st, k1. (49 sts)
Row 5: *K6, k2tog; rep from * to last st, k1. (43 sts)
Row 7: *K5, k2tog; rep from * to last st, k1. (37 sts)
Row 9: *K4, k2tog; rep from * to last st, k1. (31 sts)
Row 11: *K3, k2tog; rep from * to last st, k1. (25 sts)
Row 13: *K2, k2tog; rep from * to last st, k1. (19 sts)
Row 14: P1, [p2tog] 9 times. (10 sts)
Break yarn, leaving a tail to sew up, thread through rem sts, draw up and fasten off.

Finishing

Join seam from crown to first row of eyelets, leaving an opening of approx 10cm/4in.
Weave in ends.
Sew equal lengths of ribbon to both front edges.

BOOTEES (MAKE 2)

Using 3.75mm (US5) needles, cast on 30 sts and knit 4 rows.
Beg with row 7, work in eyelet patt to row 12.
Work rows 1–11 again.
Next row (WS): Purl.

Shape instep

Next row: K20, turn.
Next row: Sl 1, p9, turn.
Work 18 rows St st on these 10 sts, slipping first st at beg of each row.
Next row (RS): K10, pick up and knit 10 sts down side of instep, k10. (30 sts)
Next row (WS): P30, pick up and purl 10 sts down other side of instep, p10. (50 sts)
Work 10 rows St st.

Shape foot

Row 1 (RS): K1, ssk, k16, k2tog, k8, ssk, k16, k2tog, k1. (46 sts)
Work 2 rows St st.
Row 4 (WS): P1, p2tog, p14, p2tog tbl, p8, p2tog, p14, p2tog tbl, p1. (42 sts)
Row 5: K21, fold bootee in half (RS together) and cast (bind) off 2 sets of sts together in a 3-needle cast-off (bind-off).

Finishing

Sew back seam.
Weave in ends.
Thread ribbon through eyelet holes at ankles and tie in a bow.

SIZE
To fit 0–6 months

FINISHED MEASUREMENTS
Bonnet: Crown to brim 14cm/5½in **Circumference** 38cm/15in
Mittens: Length 12cm/4¾in **Circumference** 14cm/5½in
Bootees: Foot length 10cm/4in **Circumference** 14cm/5½in

MATERIALS
Yarn Wendy Merino Wool 4 ply (100% soft merino wool, 175m/191yd):
2 x 50g/1¾oz balls shade 2380 Seaspray
Needles 1 pair needles size 3mm (US2–3), 1 pair needles size 2.75mm (US2)
Notions 1m/1yd ribbon, 2.5cm/1in wide; 2m/2¼yards of ribbon, 4mm/¼in wide

TENSION (GAUGE)
28 sts and 36 rows measure 10cm/4in over pattern on 3mm (US2–3) needles
(or size needed to obtain given tension/gauge)

'Periwinkle' Bonnet, Bootees & Mittens Set

These pretty accessories were inspired by a layette set, which included
a matinée jacket and cap. It is made in an unbelievably soft Australian
merino wool that is machine washable. The fold-back brim on the bonnet is
unusual and reminiscent of the poke bonnets of the 1890s, while the shape
of the mittens and bootees has hardly changed over the centuries. Trim them
with pretty satin ribbons to give your baby an authentic vintage look.

Crisscross lace pattern
Row 1: K2, *yo, ssk, k5, k2tog, yo, k1;
rep from * to last st, k1.
Row 2: P3, *yo, p2tog, p3, p2tog tbl,
yo, p3; rep from * to end.
Row 3: K3, *k1, yo, ssk, k1, k2tog, yo,
k4; rep from * to end.
Row 4: P2, *p3, yo, p3tog, yo, p2,
p2tog, yo; rep from * to last st, p1.
Row 5: K3, *k1, k2tog, yo, k1, yo, ssk,

k4; rep from * to end.
Row 6: P3, *p2tog tbl, yo, p3, yo,
p2tog, p3; rep from * to end.
Row 7: K2, *k2tog, yo, k5, yo, ssk, k1;
rep from * to last st, k1.
Row 8: P1, p2tog, *yo, p2, p2tog, yo,
p3, yo, p3tog; rep from * to last 10 sts,
yo, p2, p2tog, yo, p3, yo, p2tog, p1.
These 8 rows form the patt.

BONNET
Using 3mm (US2–3) needles, cast on
99 sts and work 4 rows garter st (knit
every row).
Beg patt, working first and last 3 sts
of every row in garter st.
Work in patt for a total of 20 rows.
Row 21: Knit.
Row 22: K3, p93, k3.
Keeping 3 sts at each end in garter st,

and beg with a purl row, work 35 rows in St st (to form turn-back section). Work a further 8 rows in lace patt, then 4 rows in St st.

Shape crown
(From this point, do not knit the first and last sts in garter st.)

Row 1: *K8, ssk; rep from * to end, k9. *(90 sts)*

Row 2 and alt rows: Purl.

Row 3: *K7, ssk; rep from * to end. *(80 sts)*

Row 5: *K6, ssk; rep from * to end. *(70 sts)*

Cont dec in this way until 20 sts rem.

Next row: [K2tog] across row. *(10 sts)*

Break yarn, leaving a tail long enough to sew the back seam.

Thread yarn through rem sts, draw up and fasten off.

Sew a flat seam from the top to the point where crown shaping begins.

Finishing
Weave in ends. Block or press carefully as given on page 142.
Turn back brim and stitch in place.
Sew equal lengths of 2.5cm-/1in-wide ribbon to both front edges.

MITTENS (MAKE 2)
Using 2.75mm (US2) needles, cast on 43 sts and work 16 rows of lace patt as

for bonnet (without the garter-st edge). Knit 3 rows.

Row 20 (eyelet row): K1, *p1, yo, p2tog; rep from * to end.
Knit 2 rows.
Work 18 rows St st.

Shape top
Row 1 (RS): *K5, ssk; rep from * to last st, k1. *(37 sts)*

Row 2 and alt rows: Purl.

Row 3: K4, ssk; rep from * to last st, k1. *(31 sts)*

Cont dec in this way until 13 sts rem.

Next row: K1, p2tog to end. *(7 sts)*

Break yarn, leaving a tail long enough to sew the back seam.

Thread yarn through rem sts, draw up and fasten off.
Sew up seam.

Finishing
Weave in ends. Block or press carefully as given on page 142.
Thread a length of 4mm-/1/4in-wide ribbon through eyelet holes of each mitten and tie in a bow.

BOOTEES (MAKE 2)
Using 2.75mm (US2) needles, cast on 43 sts and work 20 rows of patt as for bonnet (without the garter-st edge). Knit 3 rows.

Row 24 (eyelet row): K1, *p1, yo,

p2tog; rep from * to end.
Knit 2 rows.

Row 27 (RS): K29, turn.

Row 28: P15, turn.

Work 20 rows St st on these 15 sts, slipping the first st of every row.

Next row: Sl 1, k14, pick up and knit 12 sts down side of foot, k14.

Next row: K1, p40, pick up and purl 12 sts down other side of foot, p13, k1. *(67 sts)*

Work 6 rows St st on all 67 sts.

Shape foot
Row 1: K1, ssk, k27, k2tog, k3, ssk, k27, k2tog, k1. *(63 sts)*

Row 2: K1, p2tog, p to last 3, p2tog tbl, k1. *(61 sts)*

Row 3: K1, ssk, k24, k2tog, k3, ssk, k24, k2tog, k1. *(57 sts)*

Row 4: K1, p2tog, p to last 3 sts, p2tog tbl, k1. *(55 sts)*

Row 5: K1, ssk, k21, k2tog, k3, ssk, k21, k2tog, k1. *(51 sts)*

Row 6: P25, p2tog, p to end. *(50 sts)*

Graft or cast (bind) off sts of sole tog with a 3-needle cast-off (bind-off).

Finishing
Sew back leg seam.
Block or press carefully as given on page 142.
Thread 4mm-/1/4in-wide ribbon through eyelet holes of bootees.

CRISSCROSS LACE CHART

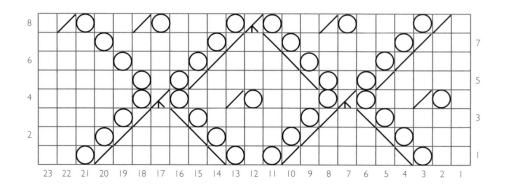

KEY

☐	RS: knit / WS: purl
◯	RS: yo / WS: yo
◸	RS: ssk / WS: p2tog tbl
◹	RS: k2tog / WS: p2tog
⋀	RS: k3tog / WS: p3tog

'Napping & Relaxing'

Comfy rompers and sleep suits

Sleeping bags and 'siren suits', like the onesie featured here (see page 64), were first introduced during the 1930s. They became popular as coveralls during the Second World War, as a means of keeping the baby warm when going into the air-raid shelter. They continued to be used after the war, as mothers realized how useful they were. These garments can be worn over a baby-gro (babysuit) or other lightweight clothes, if necessary, as an extra layer of warmth. Knitted pram suits (see page 54) made their appearance at around the same time. They consisted of separate parts – a jacket, hat and leggings with 'feet'. For babies who have started to walk, the feet can be left off and the leggings started just above the eyelet holes.

FINISHED MEASUREMENTS

Length 70cm/27½in **Width** 50cm/19½in

MATERIALS

Yarn Baruffa Cashmere (100% cashmere, 108m/118yd): 5 x 25g/1oz balls shade Storm Grey
Needles 1 pair needles size 4mm (US6)

TENSION (GAUGE)

24 sts and 36 rows measure 10cm/4in over pattern on 4mm (US6) needles
(although tension/gauge is not vital for this item)

'Valerian' Pram Blanket

The growing popularity of the pram (buggy) from the 1920s onwards meant there was an increasing need for a small, custom-sized blanket to replace the blanket borrowed from the cot (crib). As it was the top layer, in full view, it had to be something special. The pattern seen most was based on the Victorian quilt known as the English Garden, with a raised leaf at the corner of each square. This one, in flag stitch, is less complex, but the pure cashmere yarn makes it special.

Cast on 118 sts and work 17 rows garter st (knit every row).
Beg patt:
Row 1 (RS): Knit.
Row 2 (WS): K11, *k7, p1; rep from * 12 times, k11.
Row 3 (RS): K11, *k2, p6; rep from * 12 times, k11.
Row 4 (WS): K11, *k5, p3; rep from * 12 times, k11.
Row 5 (RS): K11, *k4, p4; rep from * 12 times, k11.
Row 6 (WS): K11, *k3, p5; rep from * 12 times, k11.
Row 7 (RS): K11, *k6, p2; rep from * 12 times, k11.
Row 8 (WS): K11, *k1, p7; rep from * 12 times, k11.

Keeping 11 sts at beg and end of row in garter st for border, work 8 rows of patt 26 times in total.

Work 17 rows garter st.
Cast (bind) off.

Finishing

Weave in ends.
Block or press carefully as given on page 142.

FLAG STITCH CHART

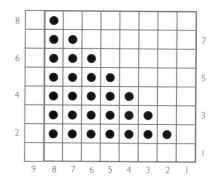

KEY

	RS: knit / WS: purl
●	RS: purl / WS: knit
	repeat

SIZE
To fit 0–6 [6–9, 9–12] months
To fit chest 41 [46, 51]cm/16 [18, 20]in

FINISHED MEASUREMENTS
Jacket: **Actual chest size** 46 [53, 57]cm/18 [21, 22½]in **Length (to back neck)** 25 [29, 33]cm/10 [11½, 13]in **Sleeves** 16 [18, 19]cm/6½ [7, 7½]in
Leggings: Length 43 [45, 48]cm/17 [18, 19]in **Hips** 46 [51, 56]cm/18 [20, 22]in
Helmet: Circumference 35.5 [41, 47]cm/14 [16, 18]in

MATERIALS
Yarn Drops Karisma (100% wool, 100m/109yd): 7 [8, 9] x 50g/1¾oz balls shade 60 Petrol Blue
Needles 1 pair needles size 3.75mm (US5), 1 pair needles size 3mm (US2–3), 1 stitch holder
Notions 7 buttons, 1.5cm/⅝in diameter; 40cm/16in elastic, 1cm/⅜in wide; 75cm/30in ribbon, 2cm/¾in wide

TENSION (GAUGE)
23 sts and 32 rows measure 10cm/4in over pattern on 3.75mm (US5) needles
(or size needed to obtain given tension/gauge)

'Comfrey' Pram Suit

It has long been believed that a child who spends a lot of time outdoors is healthier than one who stays in all day. This theory was adhered to by many mothers, who would leave their baby to sleep in the pram (buggy) outside in all weathers. But the baby wouldn't sleep if it was cold, so on top of the baby-gro (babysuit) went a pair of long, knitted leggings, a jacket, a hat and often a pair of mittens. This design is typical of those seen in the 1940s and 1950s and is still ideal for taking a baby out in the pushchair (stroller) on a cold day.

JACKET
Back
Using 3.75mm (US5) needles, cast on 53 [61, 65] sts and work 8 rows garter st (knit every row).
Beg patt:
Row 1: K2, p1 *k3, p1; rep from * to last 2 sts, k2.
Row 2: Purl.

Row 3: P1 *k3, p1; rep from * to end.
Row 4: Purl.
Rep these 4 rows until work measures 15 [18, 20]cm/6 [7, 8]in, ending after a WS row.

Shape armhole
Cast (bind) off 3 sts at beg of next

2 rows. *(47 [55, 59] sts)*
Row 3: K1, ssk, patt to last 3 sts, k2tog, k1. *(45 [53, 57] sts)*
Row 4: K1, p to last st, k1.
Rep these 2 rows until 19 [23, 23] sts rem.
Cast (bind) off.

Next row (RS): Patt to last 3 sts, k2tog, k1. *(30 [36, 40] sts)*
Next row: K1, patt to end.
Rep last 2 rows to 23 [28, 30] sts, ending after a WS row.

Shape front neck
Next row (RS): Cast (bind) off 8 [10, 12] sts, patt to last 3 sts, k2tog, k1. *(14 [17, 17] sts)*
Next row: K1, patt to end.
Keeping patt correct, cont to dec at armhole edge on next and every alt row, and at same time cast (bind) off 2 sts at neck edge on next and foll 2 [3, 3] alt rows. *(4 [5, 5] sts)*
Next row (WS): Work 1 row in patt. Dec 1 at neck edge of next row. *(3 [4, 4] sts)*
Next row: K1, p2 [3, 3].
Next row: K2tog, k1 [2, 2]. *(2 [3, 3] sts)*
Next row: K1, p1 [2, 2].
Next row (first size): K2tog and fasten off.
Next row (second and third size): K2tog, k1. *(2 sts)*
Next row (second and third size): P2tog and fasten off.

Left front (for a boy's coat)
Using 3.75mm (US5) needles, cast on 34 [40, 44] sts and work 8 rows garter st.
Work in patt:
Row 1: K2, p1, *k3, p1; rep from * to last 15 [21, 21] sts, k to end.
Row 2: K15 [21, 21], p to end.
Row 3: P1, *k3, p1; rep from * to last 17 [23, 23] sts, k to end.
Row 4: As row 2.
**Rep these 2 rows until work measures 9 [9, 11]cm/3½ [3½, 4½]in, ending with RS row.
Next row (buttonhole row): K2, cast (bind) off 2 sts, k8 [14, 14], cast (bind) off 2 sts, patt to end.

Right front (for a boy's coat)
Using 3.75mm (US5) needles, cast on 34 [40, 44] sts and work 8 rows garter st.
Work in patt:
Row 1: K15 (21, 21), *p1, k3; rep from * to last 3 sts, p1, k2.
Row 2: P19 (19, 23), k to end.
Row 3: K17 (23, 23) *p1, k3; rep from * to last st, p1.
Row 4: As row 2.*

Cont in patt as set until work measures same as back to armholes, ending with a RS row.
For a girl's coat, work as right front to *, then follow instructions given in left front from ** to ** for buttonholes, making them at the beg of a RS row.

Shape armhole
Next row (WS): Cast (bind) off 3 sts, patt to end. *(31 [37, 41] sts)*

Next row: Work in patt, casting on 2 sts over those cast (bound) off.

Make 2 more sets of buttonholes 5 [6, 7]cm/2 [2½, 3]in apart and shaping raglan as for right front when work measures same as back to armholes.**

Sleeves (make 2)

Using 3.75mm (US5) needles, cast on 25 [29, 33] sts and work 8 rows garter st.
Patt as for back, inc 1 st at each end every 5th [6th, 6th] row to 39 [43, 47] sts.
Cont without shaping until sleeve measures 16 [18, 19]cm/6½ [7, 7½]in, ending with a WS row.
Shape top as for back until 5 sts rem.
Cast (bind) off.

Collar

Using 3.75mm (US5) needles, cast on 53 [61, 65] sts and work 6 rows garter st.
Keeping 4 sts at each end in garter st, work centre sts in patt as for back for 5 [6, 7]cm/2 [2½, 3]in.
Cast (bind) off.

Finishing

Set in sleeves, then sew up side and sleeve seams.
Sew on collar starting and finishing approx halfway along front edgings.
Sew on 6 buttons.
Block or press carefully as given on page 142.

LEGGINGS

(Worked from the top down.)

Right leg

**Using 3mm (US2–3) needles, cast on 54 [60, 66] sts and work 4 rows [k1, p1] rib.
Next row: Rib 3, *yo, k2tog, rib 4; rep from * to last 3 sts, yo, k2tog, p1.
Work 3 more rows rib. **
Change to 3.75mm (US5) needles.

Shape back

Row 1: K8 [9, 10], w & t.
Row 2: Purl.
Row 3: K16 [18, 20] picking up the wrap on the previous row, w & t.
Row 4: Purl.
Row 5: K24 [27, 30] picking up the wrap on the previous row, w & t.
Row 6: Purl.
Row 7: K32 [36, 40] picking up the wrap on the previous row, w & t.
Row 8: Purl.
##Cont in St st inc 1 st at beg of next and every foll 6th row to 58 [65, 72] sts.
Then, cont to inc on back edge as set, also inc 1 st at front edge on every 6th row to 68 [75, 82] sts.
Inc 1 st at each end of next 3 rows.
(74 [81, 88] sts)

Shape leg

Cont in St st.
Dec 1 st at each end of every row until 64 [71, 78] sts rem.
Dec 1 st at each end of every alt row until 46 [53, 60] sts rem.
Dec 1 at each end of every 3rd row until 30 [33, 36] sts rem.
Cont without shaping until leg measures 16 [18, 20]cm/6½ [7½, 8]in.

Start foot

Make holes for ribbon (optional).
Next row: K2, *yo, k2tog, k1; rep from * to last st, k1.
Next row: Purl. ##

Shape instep

Row 1: K27 [30, 33], turn.
Row 2: P9 [10, 12], turn.

++Leaving the first 18 [20, 21] and last 3 sts on the needles unworked, work 12 [14, 16] rows St st on these 9 [10, 12] sts.
Dec 1 st at each end of next 2 rows.
(5 [6, 8] sts)
Break off yarn and leave sts on a holder.
With RS facing, rejoin yarn to the point where the instep meets the foot.
Next row: Pick up and knit 10 [12, 14] sts from first side of instep, k5 [6, 8] from holder, pick up and knit 10 [12, 14] sts from second side of instep, k to end. *(46 [53, 60] sts)*
Work 5 rows St st, beg with a p row. ++

Shape foot

Row 1: K5 [6, 7], k2tog, k1, ssk, k16 [19, 21], k2tog, k5 [6, 8], ssk, k11 [13, 15] to end. *(42 [49, 56] sts)*
Row 2 and alt rows: Purl.
Row 3: K4 [5, 6], k2tog, k1, ssk, k14 [17, 19], k2tog, k5 [6, 8], ssk, k10 [12, 14] to end. *(38 [45, 52] sts)*
Row 5: K3 [4, 5], k2tog, k1, ssk, k12 [15, 17], k2tog, k5 [6, 8], ssk, k9 [11, 13] to end. *(34 [41, 48] sts)*
Row 6: Purl.
Cast (bind) off.

Left leg

As for right leg from ** to **.
Change to 3.75mm (US5) needles and knit 1 row.
Row 1: P8 [9, 10], w & t.
Row 2: Knit.
Row 3: P16 [18, 20] picking up the wrap on the previous row, w & t.
Row 4: Knit.
Row 5: P24 [27, 30] picking up the wrap on the previous row, w & t.
Row 6: Knit.
Row 7: P32 [36, 40] picking up the wrap on the previous row, w & t.
Row 8: Knit.
Work from ## to ## as on right leg.

Shape instep
Next row (RS): K12 [13, 15], turn.
Next row: P9 [10, 12], turn.
Work from ++ to ++ as on right foot.

Shape foot
Row 1: K11 [13, 15], k2tog, k5 [6, 8], ssk, k16 [19, 21], k2tog, k1, ssk, k to end. *(42 [49, 56] sts)*
Row 2 and alt rows: Purl.
Row 3: K10 [12, 14], k2tog, k5 [6, 8], ssk, k14 [17, 19], k2tog, k1, ssk, k to end. *(38 [45, 52] sts)*
Row 5: K9 [11, 13], k2tog, k5 [6, 8], ssk, k12 [15, 17], k2tog, k1, ssk, k to end. *(34 [41, 48] sts)*
Row 6: Purl.
Cast (bind) off.

Finishing
Block or press carefully as given on page 142.
Join seams at centre back and front, then inside legs and crotch, then base of feet.
Weave in ends.
Thread elastic through holes at waist and thread ribbon through eyelet holes at ankles, if required.

HELMET
Ear flaps
Using 3.75mm (US5) needles, cast on 7 sts.
Row 1: *K1, p1; rep from * to last st, k1.
Row 2: *P1, k1; rep from * to last st, p1.
Row 3 (buttonhole row): Rib 3, yo, k2tog, rib to end.
Cont in rib until work measures 4cm/1½in from beg, ending with a row 2.
Row 1: K1, p1, inc in next st, rib to last 3 sts, inc in next st, rib to end. *(9 sts)*
Row 2: P1, k2, rib to last 3 sts, k2, p1.
Row 3: As row 1. *(11 sts)*

Row 4: P1, *k1, p1; rep from * to end.
Rep last 4 rows to 19 [23, 27] sts.
Work 6 rows in rib.
Break yarn and leave sts on a holder.
Work another ear flap to match, omitting buttonhole.

Main part
Using 3.75mm (US5) needles, cast on 10 sts, rib across left ear flap, cast on 31 [35, 37] sts, rib across right ear flap, cast on 10 sts. *(89 [101, 111] sts)*
Work 5 rows in rib.
Work in patt as for back of coat for 8 [9, 10]cm/3 [3½, 4]in, ending with a WS row.

Shape crown
Row 1: K1, *k2tog, k6 [8, 8]; rep from * to end. *(78 [91, 100] sts)*
Row 2 and alt rows: Purl.
Row 3: K1, *k2tog, k5 [7, 7]; rep from * to end. *(67 [81, 89] sts)*
Row 5: K1, *k2tog, k4 [6, 6]; rep from * to end. *(56 [71, 78] sts)*
Cont dec in this way to 23 [21, 23] sts, ending after a WS row.
Next row: K1, *k2tog; rep from * to end. *(12 [11, 12] sts)*
Break yarn, thread through rem sts, draw up and fasten off.

Finishing
Join back seam. Sew on button.

SIZE
To fit 0–6 months

FINISHED MEASUREMENTS
Chest 61cm/24in **Length (to back neck)** 71cm/28in
Circumference 81cm/32in **Sleeves** 15cm/6in

MATERIALS
Yarn King Cole Merino Blend DK (100% pure new wool, 112m/123yd):
8 x 50g/1¾oz balls shade Aran 46
Needles 1 pair needles size 3.25mm (US3), 1 pair needles size 4mm (US6),
tapestry needle, crochet hook size 3.5mm (USE/4), 3 stitch holders
Notions 7 buttons, 1.5cm/½in diameter; embroidery floss, if required

TENSION (GAUGE)
22 sts and 28 rows measure 10cm/4in over St st on 4mm (US6) needles
(or size needed to obtain given tension/gauge)

'Clover' Sleeping Bag

At the beginning of the twentieth century, with swaddling no longer
fashionable, babies were often put into a sleeping bag with their nightclothes
underneath. Unlike an adult sleeping bag, this garment usually had sleeves
and fastened at the bottom or down the front so that the baby could easily
have its nappy (diaper) changed. Sometimes the sleeping bag had a hood to
keep the head warm. This one doesn't have a hood, but it is still perfect for
cold nights, and is nice and roomy so that baby can still do some kicking
without getting tangled up in the bedcovers. The yarn is washable, too.

Back
Using 3.25mm (US3) needles, cast on
88 sts and work 12 rows garter st
(knit every row).
Change to 4mm (US6) needles and
work in St st until work measures
56cm/22in, ending with a WS row.
Dec row (RS): K5, k2tog, [k2, k2tog]
19 times, k5. (68 sts)

Yoke
Row 1 (WS): [K2, p1] to last 2 sts, k2.
Row 2 (RS): [P2, k1] to last 2 sts, p2.
Rep these 2 rows once more, and then
row 1 once more.

Shape armholes, keeping
pattern correct
Next row (RS): Cast (bind) off 4 sts
at beg of next 2 rows. (60 sts)
Dec 1 st at each end of every alt row

until 50 sts rem.
Cont without shaping until work
measures 10cm/4in from beg of
yoke patt.

Shoulders
Next row (RS): Cast (bind) off
5 sts at beg of next 4 rows, and 6 sts
at beg of foll 2 rows. (18 sts)
Place rem 18 sts on a holder and
break yarn.

Front

Using 3.25mm (US3) needles, cast on 88 sts and work 6 rows garter st.

Next row (buttonhole row):
K4, [yo, k2tog, k24] 3 times, yo, k2tog, k to end.
Work 5 rows garter st.
Change to 4mm (US6) needles and cont in St st until work measures 58.5cm/23in from beg.
Next row (dec row, RS): K5, k2tog, [k2, k2tog] 19 times, k5. (68 sts)
Work 5 rows of yoke patt.

Shape armholes and divide for neck

Next row (RS): Cast (bind) off 4 sts at beg of next row, work 30 sts in patt and turn.
Cont on these 30 sts, shaping armhole as on back until 25 sts rem.
Cont without shaping until armhole measures 6cm/2½in, ending with a RS row.

Shape neck

Next row (WS): Work 5 sts in patt and leave on holder, patt to end of row.
Dec 1 st at neck edge on every row until 16 sts rem.
Cont until work measures same as back to shoulders, ending with a WS row.

Next row (RS): Cast (bind) off 5 sts at beg next and foll alt row.
Work 1 row.
Cast (bind) off rem 6 sts.

Return to rem sts, rejoin yarn and work right side of front to match.

Sleeves (make 2)

Using 3.25mm (US3) needles, cast on 32 sts and work 8 rows garter st.
Next row (inc row): K3, [kfb in next st, k4] 5 times, kfb in next st, k to end. (38 sts)
Change to 4mm (US6) needles and work in yoke patt, inc 1 st at each end of every 6th row to 50 sts. Cont without shaping until sleeve measures 15cm/6in, ending with a WS row.

Shape top

Cast (bind) off 4 sts at beg of next 2 rows. (42 sts)
Dec 1 st at each end of next and every foll alt row until 32 sts rem.
Cast (bind) off 3 sts at beg of next 8 rows. (8 sts)
Cast (bind) off rem 8 sts.

Collar

Using 3.25mm (US3) needles and with RS facing, k5 from holder, pick up and knit 14 sts from right front neck edge, 1 st from right shoulder, 18 sts from back neck holder, 1 st from left shoulder, 14 sts down left front neck edge, and 5 sts from holder. (58 sts)
Work 9 rows garter st.
Cast (bind) off.

Crochet edging

Starting just below collar, and using 3.5mm (USE/4) hook, work 15dc (sc) along left front edge.
Fasten off.
Starting at bottom of opening, work 15dc (sc) along right front edge, turn.
*4ch, miss 1dc (sc), 1dc (sc) into each of next 4 sts; rep from * once more, 4ch, miss 1dc (sc), 1dc (sc) in each st to end.
Fasten off.

Finishing

Using a flat seam, join shoulders.
Set in sleeves.
Join side and sleeve seams.
Place right front edging over left front edging and sew in place at base of opening.
Weave in all ends.
Sew on buttons.
Embroider if required.
Block or press carefully as given on page 142.

SIZE
To fit 3–6 [6–9, 9–12] months

FINISHED MEASUREMENTS
Actual chest size 46 [48, 51]cm/18 [19, 20]in **Length (from back neck to crotch)** 31 [33, 37]cm/12 [13, 14½]in **Sleeves** 16.5 [18, 19]cm/6½ [7, 7½]in **Inside leg** 18 [19, 20]cm/7 [7½, 8]in

MATERIALS
Yarn Debbie Bliss Rialto DK (100% merino wool, 105m/115yd): 5 [6, 7] × 50g/1¾oz balls shade 33 Charcoal
Needles 1 pair needles size 4mm (US6), 1 pair needles size 3.25mm (US3), 1 stitch holder
Notions 1 zip (zipper), 25cm/10in long

TENSION (GAUGE)
28 sts and 28 rows measure 10cm/4in over pattern on 4mm (US6) needles (or size needed to obtain given tension/gauge)

'Tansy' Hooded Onesie

Late in the eighteenth century the idea developed that baby clothing and bedding interfered with normal exercise and prevented a baby from changing position in the pram (buggy) or cot (crib). Babies were no longer wrapped in swaddling clothes, but dressed in garments that didn't restrict their movement. Both boys and girls would wear one-piece suits indoors and outdoors. This contemporary-looking ribbed onesie is based on a pattern from the 1950s. Knitted in 100 per cent merino wool and with a practical zip- (zipper-) front fastening, it is both warm and comfortable to wear.

Legs
Using 3.25mm (US3) needles, cast on 39 [41, 45] sts.
Row 1: [K1, p1] to last st, k1.
Row 2: [P1, k1] to last st, p1.
Rep these 2 rows 3 times more then row 1 again.
Next row (inc row): P3 [2, 3], *inc in next st, p1; rep from * to last 2 [1, 2] sts, p to end. *(56 [60, 65] sts)*
Change to 4mm (US6) needles.
Row 1 (RS): Knit.
Row 2: [K1, p1] to end.
These 2 rows form the patt.
Rep these 2 rows until leg measures 18 [19, 20]cm/7 [7½, 8]in, ending with a row 2.
Break yarn and leave sts on a holder.

Work a second leg in the same way but do not break off yarn at end.

Body
Using the needle with the sts of the second leg, cast on and knit 3 sts, k56 [60, 65] of right leg, cast on 6 sts, k56 [60, 65] of left leg from holder, cast on 3 sts. *(124 [132, 142] sts)*

Cont in patt for 13 [14, 15]cm/
5 [5½, 6]in, ending with a row 2.

Shape back
Row 1: K89 [95, 103], w & t.
Row 2: Patt 54 [58, 63], w & t.
Row 3: K46 [50, 55], w & t.
Row 4: Patt 38 [42, 47], w & t.
Row 5: K30 [34, 39], w & t.
Row 6: Patt 22 [26, 31], w & t.
Row 7: Knit, picking up wraps as you
go and knitting them tog with stitch
on needle.
Row 8: Patt to end, picking up wraps
as before. *(124 [132, 142] sts)*

Waist
Change to 3.25mm (US3) needles and
work 6 rows [k1, p1] rib.

Upper body
Change back to 4mm (US6) needles
and work in patt until body measures
20 [23, 25]cm/8 [9, 10]in from crotch,
ending with a WS row.

Divide for fronts and back
Left front
Next row (RS): K31 [33, 36], turn.

Shape armhole
Next row: Cast (bind) off 4 [5, 5] sts,
work to end. *(27 [28, 31] sts)*
Keeping in patt, dec 1 st at armhole
edge of next 4 [5, 6] rows.
(23 [23, 25] sts)
Cont in patt until armhole measures
5 [5, 6]cm/2 [2, 2½]in, ending after
a WS row.

Shape neck
Next row (RS): Cast (bind) off 4
[4, 5] sts, k to end. *(19 [19, 20] sts)*
Dec 1 st at neck edge of every row
until 11 [11, 12] sts rem.

Cont until armhole measures
10 [10, 11]cm/4 [4, 4½]in, ending
with a RS row.

Shape shoulder
Next row (WS): Cast (bind) off
6 [6, 6] sts at beg of next row, and
5 [5, 6] sts on foll alt row.

Back
With RS facing, rejoin yarn to rem sts.
Cast (bind) off 4 [5, 5] sts, work 58
[61, 65] sts, turn.
Cast (bind) off 4 [5, 5] sts, work to end.
(54 [56, 60] sts)
Dec 1 st at each end of next 4 [5, 6]
rows. *(46 [46, 48] sts)*
Cont in patt without shaping until
work measures same as left front
to shoulder.

Shape shoulders
Next row (RS): Cast (bind) off 6
[6, 6] sts at beg of next 2 rows, and
5 [5, 6] sts on foll 2 rows.
Place rem 24 sts on a holder for
back neck.

Right front
With RS facing, rejoin yarn to rem
31 [33, 36] sts and work to match left
front, reversing shapings for armhole
and neck.
Join shoulder seams.

Neckband and hood
With RS facing and using 3.25mm
(US3) needles, pick up and knit 4 [4,
5] sts from cast-off (bound-off) sts at
right neck edge, 17 sts along right front,
k24 from back neck holder, 17 sts along
left front, and 4 [4, 5] sts from left neck
edge. *(66 [66, 68] sts)*
Work 6 rows in [k1 p1] rib.
Change to 4mm (US6) needles.

Next row (inc row, WS): P2, *inc in
next st, p5 [5, 4]; rep from * to last
4 [4, 6], inc in next st, k to end.
(77 [77, 81] sts)
Next row: Knit.
Next row: K5, rib to last 5, k5.
Rep last 2 rows until hood measures
13 [14, 15]cm/5¼ [5½, 6]in from
neckband.
Cast (bind) off 4 sts at beg of next
12 rows.
Cast (bind) off rem 29 [30, 33] sts.

Sleeves (make 2)
Using 3.25mm (US3) needles, cast
on 34 [36, 38] sts and work 8 rows
[k1, p1] rib.
Change to 4mm (US6) needles and
work in patt, inc 1 st at each end of
every 4th row to 50 [56, 60] sts, ending
with a WS row.
Cont without shaping until sleeve
measures 16.5 [18, 19]cm/6½ [7, 7½]in.
Next row (RS): Cast (bind) off 4
[4, 5] sts at beg of next 2 rows.
(42 [48, 50] sts)
Dec 1 st at each end of next 6 [8, 8]
rows. *(30 [32, 34] sts)*
Cast (bind) off rem sts.

Finishing
Block or press carefully as given on
page 142.
Set in sleeves, then sew up sleeve
and inside leg seams.
Insert zip (zipper).

SIZE
To fit 6–12 months

FINISHED MEASUREMENTS
Romper Suit: Length (excluding straps) 38cm/15in
Cardigan: Chest 48cm/19in **Length (to back neck)** 23cm/9in **Sleeves** 16.5cm/6½in

MATERIALS
Yarn Debbie Bliss Baby Cashmerino (55% wool, 33% microfibre,
12% cashmere, 125m/137yd): 6 x 50g/1¾oz balls shade 01 Primrose
Needles 1 pair needles size 3.25mm (US3), 1 pair needles size 2.75mm (US2),
4 stitch markers or safety pins
Notions 6 buttons, 1.5cm/⅝in diameter; 2 snap fasteners

TENSION (GAUGE)
24 sts and 42 rows measure 10cm/4in over smock pattern on 3.25mm (US3) needles
(or size needed to obtain given tension/gauge)

SPECIAL STITCH
K1US Slip RH needle under loose strands and knit next st, lifting strands over the back of this stitch

'Dandelion' Romper Suit & Cardigan

A two-piece romper suit like this one is ideal for babies who are getting a little more independent. Romper suits first became popular in America early in the twentieth century, when the trend for swaddling babies had waned, and this pattern dates from the 1940s. The dungarees-style suit can be worn without the cardigan when the weather is warm, or layered over a little cotton top on cooler days. The stitch is an interesting one, giving the impression of smocking that was so popular for Victorian children's clothing.

Smock pattern
Row 1 (RS): K1, *yf, sl 3, yb, k3; rep from * to last 4 sts, yf, sl 3, yb, k1.
Row 2 and every alt row: Purl.
Row 3: As row 1.

Row 5: K2, *k1US, k5; rep from * to last 3 sts, k1US, k2.
Row 7: K4, *yf, sl 3, yb, k3; rep from * to last st, k1.
Row 9: As row 7.

Row 11: K5, *k1US, k5; rep from * to end.
Row 12: Purl.

ROMPER SUIT
Front

Using 2.75mm (US2) needles, cast on 11 sts and work 6 rows garter st (knit every row).

Change to 3.25mm (US3) needles and work in smock patt for 2 rows.

Rows 8–17: Cast on 6 sts at beg of row, patt to end. *(71 sts)*

Cont in patt without shaping until work measures 23cm/9in.

Change to 2.75mm (US2) needles and work in [k1, p1] rib for 5cm/2in, ending with a RS row.

Next row (dec row): Rib 12 sts, *p2tog, p1, k1; rep from * 12 times, rib to end. *(59 sts)*

Change to 3.25mm (US3) needles and work 5cm/2in in smock patt, ending with a WS row.

Shape armholes

Next row (RS): [K1, p1] rib 12 sts, patt to last 12 sts, [k1, p1] rib to end. Rep last row 5 times more.

Next 2 rows: Cast (bind) off 6 sts, patt to end. *(47 sts)*

Next row: [K1, p1] rib 6 sts, patt to last 6 sts, [k1, p1] rib to end. Rep last row 5 times more.

Next row (RS): [K1, p1] rib across row to end. Rep last row 7 times more. **

Cast (bind) off.

Back

As for front to **.

Next row (RS): Rib 6 sts, cast (bind) off 35 sts, rib 6 sts to end.

Work in rib on the last set of 6 sts until strap measures 12cm/4¾in.

Next row (buttonhole): P2, p2tog, yo, p2.

Rib 3 rows.

Cast (bind) off.

Rejoin yarn to other strap and work to match.

Finishing

Weave in ends.

Block or press carefully as given on page 142.

Sew up side seams.

Sew on one button at each shoulder.

Sew on 2 snap fasteners at crotch.

CARDIGAN
Back

Using size 2.75mm (US2) needles, cast on 53 sts and work 4cm/1¾in [k1, p1] rib.

Change to 3.25mm (US3) needles and work in smock patt until work measures 23cm/9in.

Cast (bind) off.

Left front

Using 2.75mm (US2) needles, cast on 29 sts and work in rib as for back. Change to 3.25mm (US3) needles.

Cont in smock patt until work measures 12.5cm/5in, ending with a WS row.

Shape front neck slope

Dec 1 st (k2tog) at neck edge (end of row) on next and every foll 4th row until 18 sts rem.

Cont without shaping until work measures same length as back.

Cast (bind) off.

Right front

As for left front, reversing shaping, working ssk at the neck edge (beg) of a dec row.

Sleeves (make 2)

Using 2.75mm (US2) needles, cast on 37 sts and work in rib as for back, inc to 41 sts on last row as follows:

Next row: K1, kfb, k10, kfb, k11, kfb, k10, kfb, k1. *(41 sts)*

Change to 3.25mm (US3) needles and cont in patt, inc 1 st (kfb) at each end of 5th and every foll 4th row to 53 sts.

Cont without shaping until work measures 16.5cm/6½in.

Cast (bind) off.

Join shoulder seams.

Button band

Mark position for 4 buttons with safety pins, on whichever side is desired.

Starting at the bottom of the right front and with RS facing, pick up and knit 40 sts up to beg of neck shaping; 34 sts up right neck to shoulder; 22 sts across back neck; 34 sts down left neck to beg of shaping; and 40 sts down left front. *(166 sts)*

Work [k1, p1] rib for 8 rows, making buttonholes on row 4 as follows:

Buttonhole row: *Rib to marker, yo, k2tog; rep from * 4 times, rib to end.

Cast (bind) off.

Finishing

Weave in ends.

Block or press carefully as given on page 142.

Set in sleeves, then sew up side and sleeve seams.

Sew on buttons.

'Everyday Play'

Cute cardigans and cover-ups

By the 1930s baby boys were wearing some form of short trousers (pants), which meant that they needed something on their top half, too. Girls' dresses for every day were short, loose and usually made of cotton, so a cardigan was worn over the top on cooler days. Interest in knitting had grown enormously and yarn manufacturers created patterns for every level of skill they could think of. Lace, texture and stranded colour work were all popular designs for cardigans with some sort of pattern above the welt, and these were produced by every company. There were even patterns for sun suits to be topped by a cardigan or sweater, as in this yacht-patterned set (see opposite and page 78).

SIZE
To fit 9–12 [12–18] months
To fit chest 46 [52]cm/18 [20]in

FINISHED MEASUREMENTS
Actual chest size 48 [53]cm/19 [21]in
Length (to back neck) 23 [26]cm/9 [10]in

MATERIALS
Yarn Wendy Air (70% kid mohair, 30% nylon, 200m/218yd): 3 x 25g/1oz balls shade 2618 Eva (yarn is used double throughout)
Needles 1 pair needles size 4mm (US6), 1 pair needles size 3.25mm (US3), 1 circular needle size 3.25mm (US3)

TENSION (GAUGE)
20 sts and 28 rows measure 10cm/4in over St st on 4mm (US6) needles with yarn used double (or size needed to obtain given tension/gauge)

'Fritillary' Bolero

In 1947 Dior's New Look marked a departure from the restrictive and frugal fashions of the wartime. Skirts for girls, just like those of their mothers, were now longer and more voluminous. Cardigans, which typically ended below the waist, were no longer suitable to wear with such a style and so were designed to be shorter, often ending above the waist. The bolero became the must-have top of the 1950s and was often knitted in stocking (stockinette) stitch using a fluffy angora. This one has a simple all-over lace pattern and it is knitted in a fine mohair yarn, used double.

Lace pattern
Row 1 (RS): Knit.
Row 2 and alt rows: K2, *p4, k2; rep from * to end.
Row 3: *K2, k2tog, yo, k2; rep from * to last 2 sts, k2.
Row 5: Knit.
Row 7: *K4, yo, ssk; rep from * to last 2 sts, k2.
Row 8: K2, *p4, k2; rep from * to end.

Back
With 2 strands of yarn held together and using 4mm (US6) needles, cast on 56 [62] sts.
Work in lace patt for 12 [13]cm/ 4¾ [5]in, ending with a WS row.

Shape armhole
Cast (bind) off 3 sts at beg of next 2 rows. (50 [56] sts)
Dec 1 st at each end of every alt row 4 times. (42 [48] sts)

Cont without shaping until armhole measures 9.5 [11]cm/3¾ [4½]in, ending with a WS row.

Shape shoulder
Cast (bind) off 10 [7] sts at beg of next 2 rows and 0 [7] at beg next 2 rows.
22 [24] sts rem for back of neck.
Cast (bind) off loosely.

Right front

Using 4mm (US6) needles, cast on 8 [14] sts and work 2 rows in lace patt. Keeping patt correct, cast on 3 sts at beg of next and foll alt rows to 20 [26] sts.

Inc 1 st at same edge of foll alt rows to 26 [32] sts.

Cont in patt until piece measures same as back to armhole, ending with a RS row.

Shape armhole

Next row (WS): Cast (bind) off 3 sts at beg of row. *(23 [29] sts)*

Dec 1 st at same edge of alt rows 4 times. *(19 [25] sts)*

Keeping patt correct, cont until armhole measures 5cm/2in, ending with a WS row.

Shape neck

Next row (RS): Dec 1 st (ssk) at neck edge of next row, then every foll row 5 [8] times. *(13 [17] sts)*

Dec 1 st at neck edge of every alt row until 10 [14] sts rem.

Keeping patt correct, cont until armhole measures same as back to shoulder, ending with a RS row.

Cast (bind) off 10 [7] sts at beg of next row and 0 [7] sts on foll alt row.

Left front

Work as for right front, reversing shapings.

Sleeves (make 2)

Using 3.25mm (US3) needles, cast on 25 [37] sts and work 2.5cm/1in in [k1, p1] rib, inc 1 st at end of last row. *(26 [38] sts)*

Change to 4mm (US6) needles and cont in lace patt as for back.

Keeping patt correct, inc 1 st at each end of 3rd row, then every foll 4th row to 30 [40] sts.

Cont without shaping until sleeve measures 7cm/3in, ending with a WS row.

Shape top

Cast (bind) off 3 sts at beg of next 2 rows. *(24 [34] sts)*

Dec 1 st at each end of every 2nd row 2 [5] times. *(20 [24] sts)*

Dec 1 st at each end of every 3rd row 4 [1] times. *(12 [22] sts)*

Dec 1 st at each end of every 2nd row 2 [5] times. *(8 [12] sts)*

Cast (bind) off rem 8 [12] sts loosely.

Before starting the band, join shoulder seams, set in sleeves, then sew up side and sleeve seams.

Band

Using a 3.25mm (US3) circular needle and starting at the bottom right side seam, pick up and knit 66 [72] sts along right front edge, 22 [24] sts from back neck and 66 [72] sts down left front edge, and 56 [62] sts along bottom of the back. *(210 [230] sts)*

Work 6 rows [k1, p1] rib.

Cast (bind) off loosely.

Finishing

Weave in ends.

Block or press carefully as given on page 142.

LACE PATTERN CHART

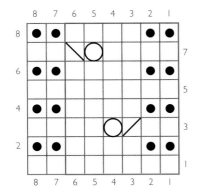

KEY

- ☐ RS: knit WS: purl
- ◯ RS: yo
- ● RS: purl WS: knit
- ◹ RS: k2tog
- ◺ RS: ssk
- ☐ repeat

'Fritillary' Bolero

SIZE
To fit 9–12 [12–18] months
To fit chest 46 [52]cm/18 [20]in

FINISHED MEASUREMENTS
Sweater: Actual chest size 50 [56]cm/20 [23]in **Length (to back neck)** 31 [36]cm/12 [14]in
Sleeves 7.5cm/3in
Shorts: Length 23 [25]cm/9 [10]in **Hips** 28 [30]cm/11 [12]in

MATERIALS
Yarn Patons 100% Cotton 4 ply (100% cotton, 331m/361yd): 2 x 100g/3½oz balls shade 1173 Pale Blue
Needles 1 pair needles size 3.25mm (US3), 1 pair needles size 2.75mm (US2), 2 stitch holders
Notions 2 buttons, 1cm/⅜in diameter; 40cm/15¾in elastic, 1cm/⅜in wide

TENSION/GAUGE
28 sts and 32 rows measure 10cm/4in over St st on 3.25mm (US3) needles
(or size needed to obtain given tension/gauge)

'Speedwell' Yachts Sun Suit

While people were very fond of taking seaside holidays (vacations), not many of them could swim. Outfits that allowed boys and girls to get some sun while paddling and playing on the beach were very popular. These shorts were originally designed to have straps over the shoulders, but I have given them an elastic waist instead, so that they are easier to put on and take off. The sun suit is knitted in cotton to be cool, comfortable and machine-washable. The yacht design is easier to knit than it looks, but you could leave it off the shorts if you prefer something a little less fancy.

SWEATER
Back
Using 2.75mm (US2) needles, cast on 71 [81] sts and work 12 rows [k1, p1] rib.
Change to 3.25mm (US3) needles and work 4 rows St st.
Work in patt from chart until work measures approx 19 [21.5]cm/7¼ [8½]in, ending with a WS row.
For second size only, work 5 sts in St st before and after the chart.

Shape armhole
Next Row (RS): Cast (bind) off 2 [4] sts at beg of next 2 rows.
(67 [73] sts)
Dec 1 st at each end of next 4 rows then foll alt rows until 57 [61] sts rem. **
Cont until armhole measures 11 [12.5]cm/4¼ [5]in, working centre boat only, ending with a WS row.

Shape shoulder
Cast (bind) off 7 [8] sts at beg of next 2 rows and 8 [8] sts at beg of foll 2 rows.
Break yarn and leave rem 27 [29] sts on a holder for back neck.

Front
Work as for back until armhole shaping is complete at **.
Cont in St st until armhole measure 6 [7]cm/2½ [3]in, ending with a WS row.

Shape neck

Next row (RS): K21 [22], sl 15 [17] sts onto a holder, k21 [22].

Cont on last set of sts, dec 1 st at neck edge on every row 6 times. *(15 [16] sts)*

Cont until work measures same as back to shoulder, ending at armhole edge.

Shape shoulder

Next row (WS): Cast (bind) off 7 [8] sts, purl to end.

Next row: Knit.

Next row: Cast (bind) off rem 8 [8] sts.

With WS facing, rejoin yarn to left side of neck and work to match.

Sleeves (make 2)

Using 2.75mm (US2) needles, cast on 39 [43] sts and work 12 rows [k1, p1] rib. Change to 3.25mm (US3) needles and work in St st, inc 1 st at each end of next and every foll 4th row to 47 [51] sts. Cont until sleeve measures 7.5cm/3in, ending with a WS row.

Shape top

Cast (bind) off 2 [4] sts at beg of next 2 rows. *(43 [43] sts)*

Dec 1 st at each end of every row 4 [0] times, then every alt row 7 [13] times. *(21 [17] sts)*

Dec 1 st at each end every row 4 [2] times. *(13 [13] sts)*

Cast (bind) off rem sts.

Join left shoulder seam.

Neckband

Using 2.75mm (US2) needles and with RS facing, knit 27 [29] sts from back neck holder, pick up and knit 15 sts from left front neck, 15 [17] sts from front neck holder, and 15 sts from right front neck. *(72 [76] sts)*

Work 6 rows [k1, p1] rib.

Cast (bind) off loosely.

Right shoulder placket

Using 2.75mm (US2) needles and with RS facing, pick up and knit 6 sts from edge of neckband, and 15 [16] sts along right front shoulder.

Knit 3 rows.

Next row (buttonhole row, RS): K3, yo, ssk, k6, yo, ssk, k to end.

Knit 2 rows.

Cast (bind) off.

Work right back shoulder to match, omitting buttonholes.

SHORTS
Front

Using 2.75mm (US2) needles, cast on 19 [23] sts and work 5cm/2in St st.

Cast on 4 sts at beg of every row to 67 [71] sts.

Change to 3.25mm (US3) needles and inc 1 st at each end of alt rows to 71 [79] sts.

Work in patt from chart as for front of sweater (completing the first two rows of boats only), inc 1 st at each end of 5th and every foll 6th row to 77 [83] sts.

YACHTS PATTERN CHART

KEY

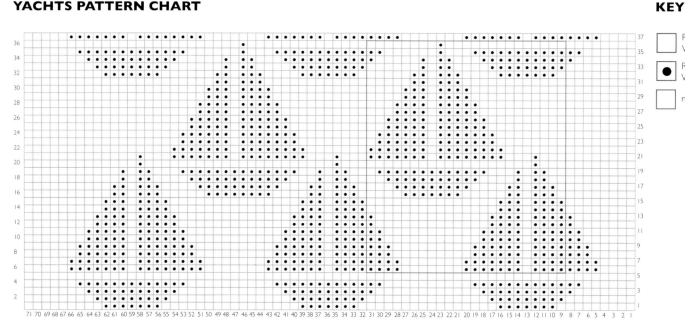

	RS: knit WS: purl
●	RS: purl WS: knit
	repeat

For second size only, work 4 sts in St st before and after the chart.

When side seam measures 15 [18]cm/ 6 [7]in, change to 2.75mm (US2) needles and work 8 rows [k1, p1] rib. Cast (bind) off loosely.

Back

Using 3.25mm (US3) needles, pick up 19 sts from cast-on row.

Cast on 4 sts at beg of every row to 67 [71] sts.

Cont as for front until side seams measure 15 [18]cm/6 [7]in, ending with a WS row.

Shape back (short rows)

Row 1: K67 [72], turn.

Row 2: P57 [62], turn.

Row 3: K47 [52], turn.

Cont in this way until p17 [22] has been worked, turn.

Next row (RS): Knit to end.

Next row (WS): P67 [72].

Change to 2.75mm (US2) needles and work in rib as for front.

Sew crotch seam.

Edgings

Using 2.75mm (US2) needles and with RS facing, start at side seam and pick up and knit 64 sts around legs.

Work 4 rows [k1, p1] rib.

Cast (bind) off loosely.

Finishing

Set in sleeves, then sew up side and sleeve seams of sweater.

Sew buttons onto right back shoulder.

Sew up side seams of shorts.

Weave in ends.

Stitch elastic to inside of waistband with herringbone stitch.

Block or press carefully as given on page 142.

SIZE
To fit 6–9 [9–12] months
To fit chest 46 [52]cm/18 [20]in

FINISHED MEASUREMENTS
Chest 48 [53]cm/19 [21]in **Length (to back neck, excluding neckband)** 22 [24.5]cm/8½ [9½]in **Sleeves** 15 [18]cm/6 [7]in

MATERIALS
Yarn Debbie Bliss Baby Cashmerino (55% wool, 33% acrylic, 12% cashmere, 125m/137yd): 3 [4] x 50g/1¾oz balls shade 102 Camel (MC), 1 x 50g/1¾oz ball shade 011 Chocolate (CC)
Needles 1 pair needles size 3mm (US2–3), 1 pair needles size 3.75mm (US5), 3 stitch holders, 4 [5] stitch markers or safety pins
Notions 4 [5] buttons, 1cm/⅜in diameter

TENSION (GAUGE)
21 sts and 31 rows measure 10cm/4in over St st on 3.75mm (US5) needles
(or size needed to obtain given tension/gauge)

'Yarrow' Teddy Bear Cardigan

By the late 1940s hundreds of women who had been knitting for the war effort had turned their attention to knitting for their families. The many wool spinners of the time published more and more patterns to attract people to buy their brand of wool. One of the most popular patterns were for children's cardigans, often featuring a motif or pattern above the hem. Flowers, vehicles, birds, animals and toys were all popular, but the teddy bear was number one.

Body
(Worked in one piece to the armholes.)
Using 3mm (US2–3) needles and MC, cast on 101 [111] sts.
Row 1: [K1, p1] to last st, k1.
Row 2: [P1, k1] to last st, p1.

Work 9 more rows in rib.
Change to 3.75mm (US5) needles and work 2 rows St st, beg with a k row.
Join in CC and work from chart for 18 rows as follows:
Front/odd rows: Work chart 9 [10] times, k2 [1].

Back/even rows: P2 [1], work chart 9 [10] times.

Break off CC and cont in MC in St st until work measures 14 [16]cm/ 5½ [6½]in, ending with a WS row.

Divide work for fronts and back
Right front
Next row (RS): K24 [26] and turn.

Shape armhole and neck
Next row (WS): Cast (bind) off 3 sts,
p to end. *(21 [23] sts)*
Next row: K1, ssk, k to last 3 sts,
k2tog, k1.
Next row: Purl.
Cont in St st, dec at armhole edge
only on every alt row and neck edge
of every 4th row until 6 [8] sts rem.
Dec at armhole edge only (on every
row) until all sts are worked off.
Fasten off.

Back

With RS facing, rejoin MC and cast
(bind) off 3 [3] sts at beg of row, k50
[56], turn. *(50 [56] sts)*

Shape armhole
Next row (WS): Cast (bind) off 3 sts,
p to end. *(47 [53] sts)*
Next row (RS): K1, ssk, k to last 3 sts,
k2tog, k1. *(45 [51] sts)*
Cont in St st, dec 1 st at both ends of
every alt row until 21 [25] sts rem.
Leave sts on a holder.

Left front

With RS facing, rejoin MC to rem
24 [26] sts, cast (bind) off 3 [3] sts.
(21 [23] sts)
Complete as for right front, reversing
shaping for front and armhole.

Sleeves (make 2)

Using 3mm (US2–3) needles and MC,
cast on 35 sts and work 11 rows [k1,
p1] rib as for body.
Change to 3.75mm (US5) needles.
Cont in St st, beg with a k row, inc
1 st at each end of first and every
foll 4th row to 47 [51] sts.

Cont without further shaping until
sleeve measures 15 [18]cm/6 [7]in,
ending with a WS row.

Shape top
Cast (bind) off 3 [3] sts at beg of next
2 rows. *(41 [45] sts)*
Next row (RS): K1, ssk, k to last 3 sts,
k2tog, k1.
Cont to dec 1 st at each end on every
alt row until 7 sts rem.
Leave sts on a holder.
Set in sleeves.

Front bands and back edging

Mark with a safety pin or removable
stitch marker places for 4 [5] evenly
spaced buttonholes on either the left
or right front (traditionally, on the left
for a boy and the right for a girl).

Using 3mm (US2–3) needle and MC,
pick up and knit 54 [59] sts up right
front, 7 sts of right sleeve, 21 [25] sts of
back, 7 sts of left sleeve and 54 [59] sts
of left front. *(143 [157] sts)*
Row 1 (WS): *P1, k1; rep from * to
last st, p1.
Row 2 (RS): *K1, p1; rep from * to
last st, k1.
Row 3: As row 1.
Row 4: *Work in rib as set until
buttonhole marker, yf, k2tog; rep from
* 4 [5] times, work in rib to end.
Rows 5–8: Work 4 rows in rib as set.
Row 9: Cast (bind) off.

Finishing

Sew sleeve seams and weave in ends.
Sew on buttons.
Block or press carefully as given on
page 142.

TEDDY PATTERN CHART   KEY

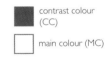

contrast colour (CC)

main colour (MC)

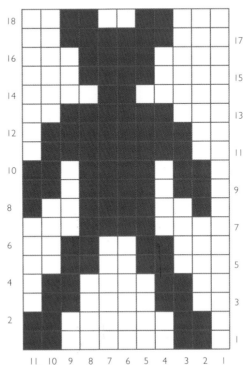

SIZE
To fit 0–6 months

FINISHED MEASUREMENTS
Chest 46cm/18in
Length (to back neck) 22cm/9in
Sleeves 13cm/5in

MATERIALS
Yarn Hjertegarn Blend Bamboo 4 ply (70% bamboo, 30% cotton, 150m/164yd):
2 x 50g/1¾oz balls shade 6007 Baby Blue
Needles 1 pair needles size 3mm (US2–3), 1 pair needles size 3.75mm (US5),
4 stitch holders
Notions 3 buttons, 7mm/¼in diameter

TENSION (GAUGE)
26 sts and 36 rows measure 10cm/4in over St st using 3.75mm (US5) needles
(or size needed to obtain given tension/gauge)

'Cornflower' Lace-Yoke Cardigan

Cardigans and jackets were popular for babies, especially ones of this shape with a yoke. This pretty example, with its unusual lace pattern, is a more ornate version than many, and the baby here looks very happy to be wearing it. This style of cardigan would have been worn by both boys and girls, so it works equally well over a baby-gro (babysuit) or pretty dress. The bodice and sleeves are in plain stocking (stockinette) stitch and the yoke pattern is not difficult, although it requires careful counting on the decrease rows.

Back
Using 3mm (US2–3) needles, cast on 78 sts and work 7 rows garter st (knit every row).
Change to 3.75mm (US5) needles and work in St st until work measures 13cm/5in, ending with a purl row.

Shape armhole
**Cast (bind) off 2 sts at beg of next 2 rows. (74 sts)
Row 3: K1, sk2po, k to last 4 sts, k3tog, k1. (70 sts)
Row 4: Purl.
Row 5: As row 3.** (66 sts)

Row 6 (WS): K6, k2tog to last 6 sts, k6. (39 sts)
Break yarn and leave sts on a holder.

Sleeves (make 2)

Using 3mm (US2–3) needles, cast on 32 sts and work 7 rows garter st. Change to 3.75mm (US5) needles and work 6 rows St st, beg with a k row. Inc 1 st at each end of next and every foll 5th row to 44 sts.

Cont without shaping until work measures 13cm/5in ending with a WS row.

Shape top as for back from ** to **. (32 sts)

Next row (dec row, WS): K1, [k2tog, k2] 7 times, k2tog, k1. (24 sts)

Break yarn and leave sts on a holder.

Left front

Using 3mm (US2–3) needles, cast on 41 sts and work 7 rows garter st. Change to 3.75mm (US5) needles.

Row 1: Knit.

Row 2: K4, p to end.

Rep these 2 rows until front measures same as back to armhole, ending at side edge **.

Shape raglan

Row 1 (RS): Cast (bind) off 2 sts, k to end. (39 sts)

Row 2 (WS): K4, p to end.

Row 3 (RS): K1, sk2po, k to end. (37 sts)

Rep rows 2 and 3 once more. (35 sts)

Next row (WS): K5, [k2tog] to last 2 sts, k2. (21 sts)

Break yarn and leave sts on a holder.

Right front

As for left front to **.

Shape raglan

Row 1 (WS): Cast (bind) off 2 sts, p to last 4, k4. (39 sts)

Row 2 (RS): K to last 4 sts, k3tog, k1. (37 sts)

Row 3 (WS): P to last 4 sts, k4.

Row 4: Rep row 2. (35 sts)

Next row (WS): K2, [k2tog] across row to last 5 sts, k5. (21 sts)

Next row (RS): Knit.

Do not break off yarn at end; leave sts on needle.

Yoke

With RS facing, slip sts of left front, first sleeve, back and second sleeve onto a 3.75mm (US5) needle. Using needle with sts of right front, knit across these 108 sts. (129 sts)

Buttonhole row (WS): K to last 3 sts, yo, ssk, k1.

Knit 3 rows.

Start yoke pattern

Row 1 and all WS rows: K4, p to last 4 sts, K4, making buttonhole on row 13.

Row 2 (RS): K8, *yo, ssk, k6; rep from * to last st, k1.

Row 4: K6, *k2tog, yo, k1, yo, ssk, k3; rep from * to last 3 sts, k3.

Row 6: K5, *k2tog, yo, k3, yo, ssk, k1; rep from * to last 4 sts, k4.

Row 8: K4, k2tog, *yo, k5, yo, sk2po; rep from * to last 11 sts, yo, k5, yo, ssk, k4.

Row 10: K5 *yo, k2, sk2po, k2, yo, k1; rep from * to last 4 sts, k4.

Row 12: K4, k2tog, *yo, k1, sk2po, k1, yo, k3tog; rep from * to last 11 sts, yo, k1, sk2po, k1, yo, k2tog, k4. (99 sts)

Row 14: K6, *yo, sk2po, yo, k3; rep from * to last 3 sts, k3.

Row 16: K6, *k2tog, yo, k4; rep from * to last 3 sts, k3.

Dec for yoke shaping

Row 17 (WS): K4, p2tog, *p3, p3tog; rep from * to last 9 sts, p3, p2tog, k4. (69 sts)

Row 18: K7, *yo, ssk, k3, k2tog, yo, k1; rep from * to last 6 sts, k6.

Row 19 and all other WS rows: K4, p to last 4 sts, k4.

Row 20: K8, *yo, ssk, k1, k2tog, yo, k3; rep from * to last 5 sts, k5.

Row 22: K9, *yo, sk2po, yo, k5; rep from * to last 4 sts, k4.

Row 24: K6, k2tog, k1, *k2tog, yo, k2, sk2po, k1; rep from * to last 12 sts, k2tog, yo, k2, ssk, k6. (55 sts)

Row 25: K4, p to last 4 sts, k4.

Change to 3mm (US2–3) needles and knit 5 rows, making a buttonhole on second row.

Cast (bind) off.

Finishing

Join raglan seams, then sew up side and sleeve seams.

Sew on buttons.

Weave in all ends.

Block or press carefully as given on page 142.

SIZE
To fit 3–6 [9–12, 12–18, 18–24] months

FINISHED MEASUREMENTS
Actual chest size 41 [46, 52, 55]cm/16½ [19, 21, 22]in
Length (to back neck) 22 [26, 29, 31]cm/9 [10½, 11½, 12½]in
Sleeves 15 [16.5, 19, 20.5]cm/6 [6½, 7½, 8]in

MATERIALS
Yarn Katia Mississippi 3 4 ply (60% cotton, 40% acrylic, 210m/230yd):
2 [3, 3, 3] x 50g/1¾oz balls shade 765 Magenta (MC), 2 [2, 2, 2] x 50g/1¾oz
balls shade 762 Lime (C1), 2 [2, 2, 3] x 50g/1¾oz balls shade 312 Ecru (C2)
Needles 1 pair needles size 3.25mm (US3), 1 pair needles size 2.75mm (US2)
Notions 3 [4, 5, 5] buttons, 1cm/⅜in diameter

TENSION (GAUGE)
28 sts and 32 rows measure 10cm/4in over St st on 3.25mm (US2) needles
(or size needed to obtain given tension/gauge)

'Willowherb' Stripy Cardigan

As fashions in children's clothes changed in the mid-twentieth century, boys were often dressed in shorts and shirts, instead of the pre-war romper suits. Cardigans became fashionable for both sexes, and this smart young man is wearing a three-quarter-sleeve cardigan knitted in cotton in a striped pattern with a difference. The original version commemorated VE Day, but I have turned the 'Vs' (for Victory) on their sides for a modern update. Knit the bands in the same colour as the hem for a variation and choose your buttons to match the stripes.

Cardigan is worked in St st throughout, except where otherwise stated for bands.

Back
Using 2.75mm (US2) needles and C1, cast on 58 [66, 74, 78] sts.
Work in [k1, p1] rib for 10 [10, 10, 12] rows.
Change to 3.25mm (US3) needles beg with 6 rows St st in MC, work stripe patt, alternating between 6 rows in MC and 8 rows of chart.
Cont until work measures 11 [14, 16, 18]cm/4½ [5½, 6½, 7]in from beg, ending with a WS row.

Shape armholes
Cont in stripe patt, cast (bind) off 2 [3, 4, 4] sts at beg of next 2 rows.
(54 [60, 66, 70] sts)

Dec 1 st at each end of alt rows 1 [1, 4, 4] times. *(52 [58, 58, 62] sts)*
Cont in patt until armhole measures 10 [11.5, 11.5, 12.5]cm/4 [4½, 4½, 5]in.

Shape shoulder
Cast (bind) off 7 [7, 7, 8] sts at beg of next 4 [4, 4, 2] rows and 0 [0, 0, 8] sts at beg of foll 2 rows. *(24 [30, 30, 30] sts)*
Cast (bind) off rem sts.

Left front

Using 2.75mm (US2) needles and C1, cast on 26 [30, 34, 36] sts.
Work 10 [10, 10, 12] rows [k1, p1] rib as for back.
Change to 3.25mm (US3) needles and work in stripe patt until work measures same as back to armholes, ending with a WS row.

Shape armhole and front slope

Cont in patt, cast (bind) off 2 [4, 4, 4] sts at beg of next row. (24 [26, 30, 32] sts)
Next row: Purl.
Dec 1 st at armhole edge on next and every alt row 1 [1, 4, 4] times, at same time dec 1 st at neck edge on next, and every foll 4th row to 14 [15, 16, 16] sts.
Cont without shaping until front measures same as back to shoulder, ending with a WS row.

Shape shoulder

Cast (bind) off 7 [8, 8, 8] sts on next row, and 7 [7, 8, 8] sts on foll alt row.

Right front

Work as for left front, reversing shaping for armhole and neck.

Sleeves

Using 2.75mm (US2) needles and MC, cast on 34 [38, 42, 46] sts and work in rib as for back.
Change to size 3.25mm (US3) needles and work in stripe patt (omitting the first 6 rows MC), inc 1 st at each end of 9th and foll 10th row to 38 [42, 46, 50] sts.
Cont without further shaping until sleeve measures 15 [16.5, 19, 20.5]cm/ 6 [6½, 7½, 8]in, ending with a WS row.

Shape cap

Cast (bind) off 2 [3, 4, 4] sts at beg of next 2 rows. (34 [36, 38, 42] sts)
Dec 1 at each end of alt rows to 12 [12, 14, 14] sts.
Cast (bind) off rem sts loosely.

Front bands

Mark position for 3 [4, 5, 5] buttons on left or right front, depending on whether for a boy or girl.
With RS facing, using MC and beg at the bottom of the right front, pick up and knit 2 sts for every 3 rows up the right front, around the back neck and down the left front.
Next 4 rows: [K1, p1] rib.
Row 5: Rib to first marker; *yo, k2tog, rib 7; rep from * 3 [4, 5, 5] times, rib to end.
Next 3 rows: [K1, p1] rib.
Cast (bind) off in rib.

Finishing

Set in sleeves, then sew up side and sleeve seams.
Sew on buttons.
Weave in ends.
Block or press carefully as given on page 142.

CHART **KEY**

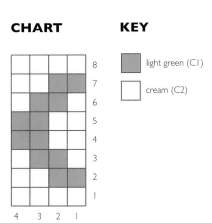

'Willowherb' Stripy Cardigan

'Dress up for the Party'

Pretty dresses for little girls

Since Kate Greenaway (1846–1901) first published her storybooks with their charming illustrations of little girls wearing high-waisted dresses with puff sleeves, frills and ribbons, such garments have been the preferred fashion for parties and special occasions. This style has the added appeal that it looks attractive whatever the skirt length, and most of the patterns included here can be made longer or shorter according to the wishes of the knitter. For everyday wear they can be knitted in a wool-mix yarn, but to make them even more 'dressy' they would look extra-special knitted in silk.

'Honeysuckle' Feather-Stitch Dress

This little dress is typical of the style and shape of babies' dresses of the late 1930s and early 1940s, with its short Empire-line yoke and grown-on sleeves. The long, gathered skirt in a simple lace pattern was also fashionable at the time for little girls who had just learned to walk. Dresses like these were worn with shoes and ankle socks (anklets), and perhaps a knitted jacket to cover the arms when going outside. The pattern has been updated here to include more than one size, and is knitted in a wool-and-cashmere yarn to span the seasons.

Back
Using 4mm (US6) needles, cast on 79 [101] sts.
Knit 4 rows.

Begin feather-stitch pattern
Row 1 (RS): K1, k2tog, k3, *yo, k1, yo, k3, k2tog, ssk, k3; rep from * to last 7 sts, yo, k1, yo, k3, ssk, k1.
Row 2 (WS): K1, p to last st, k1.
Rep these 2 rows until work measures 10cm/4in.
Change to 3.75mm (US5) needles.
Cont until work measures 20cm/8in.

Change to 3.25mm (US3) needles and work for another 2.5cm/1in, ending with a WS row.

First size
Next row (dec row): *K3, k2tog; rep from * to last 4 sts, k4. (64 sts)

Second size

Next row (dec row): K5, k2tog, *k1, k2tog, k2tog; rep from * to last 4 sts, k4. *(64 sts)*

Both sizes

Next row (WS): Purl.

Next row (eyelets row): K2, *yo, k2tog, k2; rep from * to last 2 sts, yo, k2tog.

Cont in St st for another 2.5cm/1in, ending with a WS row.

Shape armhole

Cast on 10 [16] sts at beg of next 2 rows. ** *(84 [96] sts)*

Beg with a knit row, work in St st for 15 rows.

Divide for back neck

Next row (WS): P39 [45], k3; turn, and work on these sts until armholes measure 9 [11]cm/3½ [4¼]in wide, keeping 3 sts at neck opening in garter st.

Break yarn and leave sts on a holder. Rejoin yarn to WS of rem sts and work other half of back to match. Leave sts on a holder.

Front

As back to **.

Cont in St st until armhole measures 8 [10]cm/3¼ [4]in wide, ending with a WS row.

Shape neck

Next row (RS): K26 [32], k34 and place these 32 sts on a holder, k26 [32].

Cont working on the last 26 [32] sts of right shoulder, until armhole measures 9.5 [11.5]cm/3¾ [4½]in.

Break yarn and leave sts on a holder. Rejoin yarn to WS of left shoulder and work in St st until armhole measures 9.5 [11.5]cm/3¾ [4½]in.

Graft or cast (bind) off shoulder sts tog with back sts, leaving 16 sts each side of back neck on the holder.

Neck edging

Using 3.25mm (US3) needles and beg on the left side of back neck opening, knit 16 sts from holder, 7 [9] sts down left front neck, knit across 32 sts of front neck from holder, pick up and knit 7 [9] sts from right front neck, knit 16 sts from right back neck holder.

Work 4 rows garter st, making a buttonhole on second row as follows:

Row 2: K2, yo, k2tog, k to end.

Cast (bind) off.

Sleeves (make 2)

Using 4mm (US6) needles, pick up and knit 46 [57] sts evenly along sleeve edge (approx 2 sts for every 3 rows).

Row 1 (WS): K1, p to last st, k1.

Work 5 rows in feather-stitch patt as for skirt.

Next 3 rows: Knit.

Cast (bind) off.

Finishing

Sew up side and sleeve seams.

Weave in all ends.

Block or press carefully as given on page 142.

Sew button at back neck opening.

Weave ribbon through eyelets at yoke.

SIZE

To fit 9–12 [12–18, 18–24] months
To fit chest 46 [52, 56]cm/18 [20, 22]in

FINISHED MEASUREMENTS

Actual chest size 48 [57, 61]cm/19 [22, 24]in
Length (to back neck) 40 [45, 50]cm/16 [18, 20]in

MATERIALS

Yarn Sublime Baby Cashmere Merino Silk DK (75% extra fine merino wool, 20% silk, 5% cashmere, 116m/127yd): 4 [5, 5] x 50g/1¾oz balls shade 002 Cuddle (MC), 1 x 50g/1¾oz ball shade 243 Little Miss Plum (CC)
Needles 1 pair needles size 3.75mm (US5), 1 pair needles size 3.25mm (US3)
Notions 2 buttons, 1cm/⅜in diameter

TENSION (GAUGE)

23 sts and 29 rows measure 10cm/4in over St st on 3.75mm (US5) needles (or size needed to obtain given tension/gauge)

'Bluebell' Basket-Weave Dress

This dress is made in a luxurious silk-and-wool yarn, which makes it an all-seasons dress that is not too hot for cool summer days but warm enough in the winter. It is also machine-washable, which is an added bonus for baby wear. The hem and yoke are in a simple pattern of knit and purl stitches, which makes this an ideal dress for a new knitter to make. The little flowers around the yoke and hem are not difficult to do, but they could be left off or embroidered on after the dress is finished. The shoulders are fastened with pretty buttons to make it easy to get over the baby's head.

Back

Using 3.75mm (US5) needles and MC, cast on 102 [110, 118] sts. Knit 4 rows.

Begin basket-weave pattern
Row 1 (RS): K1, *k4, p4; rep from * to last 5 sts, k5.
Row 2: K1, *p4, k4; rep from * to last 5 sts, p4, k1.

Rep these 2 rows once more.
Row 5: As row 2.
Row 6: As row 1.
Rep these last 2 rows once more.
These 8 rows form basket-weave patt.

Rep these 8 rows once, then rows 1–4 again.

Dec row: K2, *k2tog, k6; rep from * to last 4 sts, k2tog, k2. *(89 [97, 105] sts)*
Work 3 rows St st, then work 3 rows from chart A.
Cont in St st until work measures 30.5 [34, 38]cm/12 [13½, 15]in.
Next row: Dec to 54 [64, 70] sts.
Dec row, first size: K1, k2tog, *k1, [k2tog] twice; rep from * to last st, k1. *(54 sts)*
Dec row, second size: K8, k2tog, *k1, [k2tog] twice; rep from * to last 7 sts, k7. *(64 sts)*
Dec row, third size: K9, k2tog, *k1, [k2tog] twice; rep from * to last 9 sts, k9. *(70 sts)*
Purl 1 row.

Shape armhole
Cast (bind) off 4 sts at beg of next 2 rows. *(46 [56, 62] sts)*

Work 2 rows St st, then work 3 rows from chart B.
For 2nd size only: P2tog at each end of next row. *(46 [54, 62] sts)*
Row 8 (WS): Purl 1 row**.
Cont in basket-weave patt (as for hem) for 24 [28, 32] rows.
Cast (bind) off in patt.

Front

As back to **. *(46 [54, 62] sts)*
Work basket-weave patt as for hem for 12 [16, 20] rows.

Shape neck

Next row: Patt 15 [17, 21] sts, cast (bind) off 16 [20, 20] sts, patt 15 [17, 21] sts.
Cont in patt on last set of sts to same length as back, ending with a WS row.
Knit 1 row and cast (bind) off.
With WS facing, rejoin yarn and work other shoulder to match.
Join shoulder seams for 2.5cm/1in.

Sleeves

With RS facing, pick up and knit 50 [58, 66] sts along armhole edge.
Work 5 rows St st.
Dec 1 st at each end of next and every foll sixth row to 42 [46, 50] sts.
When sleeve measures 10 [12.5, 15]cm/4 [5, 6]in, change to 3.25mm (US3) needles and work in basket-weave patt for 12 [16, 16] rows.
Cast (bind) off in patt.

FINISHING

Sew up side and sleeve seams.
Weave in all ends.
Block or press carefully as given on page 142.
Sew buttons at each side of back neck and make button loops to correspond on front neck edge.

CHART A

KEY
contrast colour (CC)
RS: knit
WS: purl
repeat

CHART B

KEY
main colour (MC)
contrast colour (CC)

'Bluebell' Basket-Weave Dress

SIZE
To fit 3–6 [6–12, 12–18] months

FINISHED MEASUREMENTS
Dress: Actual chest size 41 [46, 53]cm/16 [18, 20]in
Length (to back neck) 33 [29, 43]cm/15 [17, 19]in
Bolero: Length (to back neck) 13 [15, 19]cm/5 [6, 7½]in

MATERIALS
Yarn Fyberspates Scrumptious 4 ply Sport (45% silk, 55% superwash merino wool, 365m/399yd): 2 [2, 3] x 100g/3½oz skeins Shade 315 Magenta
Needles 1 pair needles size 3.75mm (US5), 1 pair needles size 3.25mm (US3), 1 pair needles size 2.75mm (US3), 3 stitch holders
Notions 3 [3, 4] buttons for bolero and 2 for shoulder fastening on dress, 15mm/⅝in diameter

TENSION (GAUGE)
23 sts and 32 rows measure 10cm/4in over pattern on 3.75mm (US5) needles (or size needed to obtain given tension/gauge)

'Foxglove' Zigzag Dress & Bolero

Fashions for girls in the 1950s reflected those of young women. Dresses had flared skirts to just above the knee and, usually, short sleeves. Dress and bolero sets became popular when rationing ended and materials were more plentiful. They were worn for all occasions, but this one is knitted in a silk mix to make it more special. The dress fastens with buttons on the shoulders, so it is easy to get over the head.

Zigzag pattern
Row 1: K1, *k4, k2tog, yo, k1; rep from * 13 [15, 17] times, k2.
Row 2 and all alt rows: Purl.
Row 3: K1, *k3, k2tog, yo, k2; rep from * 13 [15, 17] times, k2.
Row 5: K1, *k2, k2tog, yo, k3; rep from * 13 [15, 17] times, k2.
Row 7: K1, *k1, k2tog, yo, k4; rep from * 13 [15, 17] times, k2.
Row 9: K1, *k3, yo, ssk, k2; rep from * 13 [15, 17] times, k2.
Row 11: K1, *k4, yo, ssk, k1; rep from * 13 [15, 17] times, k2.
Row 13: K1, *k5, yo, ssk; rep from * 13 [15, 17] times, k2.
Row 14: Purl.
Rep from row 3 for patt.

DRESS
Back
Using 3.25mm (US3) needles, cast on 94 [108, 122] sts and work 4 rows garter st (knit every row).
Change to 3.75mm (US5) needles and work in zigzag patt to 19 [22, 24]cm/ 9 [10½, 12½]in, ending after a WS row.
Next row (dec row): [K2tog] across row. *(47 [54, 61] sts)*
Change to 3.25mm (US3) needles and work 8 [8, 8] rows [k1, p1] rib.
Change to 3.75mm (US5) needles and purl 1 row, dec 1 st at each end.

(45 [52, 59] sts)
Work in zigzag patt from row 1 for a further 5cm/2in, ending with a WS row.

Shape armhole
Keeping patt correct, cast (bind) off 2 [3, 3] sts at beg of next 2 rows. *(41 [46, 53] sts)*
Cast (bind) off 2 sts at beg of foll 2 rows. *(37 [42, 49] sts)*
Dec 1 st at each end next row**. *(35 [40, 47] sts)*
Cont in patt until work measures 37 [42, 47]cm/14½ [16½, 18½]in.

Shape shoulder
Cast (bind) off 3 [4, 5] sts at beg next 4 rows. *(23 [24, 27] sts)*
Leave these sts on a holder for the back neck.

Front
Work as back to ** and cont in patt until work measures 33 [37, 42]cm/13 [14½, 16½]in, ending after a WS row.

Shape neck
Next row: Patt 11 [13, 15], turn.
Dec 1 st at neck edge of every row until 6 [8, 10] sts rem.
Cont in patt until work measures same as back to shoulders, keeping patt for as long as possible, or work in St st, ending with a RS row.

Shape shoulders
Cast (bind) off 3 [4, 5] sts at beg of next and foll alt row.
Return to sts for right shoulder:
Slip centre 13 [14, 17] sts onto a holder, rejoin yarn and work to match right shoulder but do not cast (bind) off, leave rem 6 [8, 10] sts on a holder.

Neckband
Join left shoulder.

With RS facing and using 3.25mm (US3) needles, knit 23 [24, 27] sts from back holder, pick up and knit 13 sts down left front neck, 13 [14, 17] sts from front holder and 13 sts from right front neck. *(62 [64, 70] sts)*
Work 4 rows garter st.
Cast (bind) off.

Right shoulder placket
Front
With WS facing and using 3.25mm (US3) needles, k6 [8, 10] sts from holder, then pick up and knit 4 from edge of neck. *(10 [12, 14] sts)*
Knit 1 row.
Next row (buttonhole row): K1 [2, 3], yo, k2tog, k3 [4, 5], yo, k2tog, k2.
Knit 2 rows.
Cast (bind) off.

Back
Pick up and knit 6 [8, 10] sts from back shoulder, and 4 sts from neck edge.
Work 4 rows garter st.
Cast (bind) off.

Finishing
Weave in ends.
Block or press carefully as given on page 142.
Sew 2 buttons onto the right shoulder.

BOLERO
Back
Using 3.25mm (US3) needles, cast on 45, [52, 59] sts and work 8 rows [k1, p1] rib.
Change to 3.75mm (US5) needles and work in zigzag patt to 6 [7.5, 7.5]cm/2½ [3, 3]in, ending with a WS row.

Shape armholes
Cast (bind) off 2 [2, 3] sts at beg next 2 rows. *(41 [48, 53] sts)*
Cast (bind) off 2 sts at beg foll 2 rows. *(37 [44, 49] sts)*

Dec 1 st at each end next row.
(35 [42, 47] sts)
Cont in patt to 9 [10, 11.5]cm/3½ [4, 4½]in from start of armhole.
Cast (bind) off 4 [5, 5] sts at beg of next 4 rows and 0 [0, 2] at beg of foll 2 rows. *(19 [22, 23] sts)*
Break yarn and leave sts on a holder.

Left front
Using 3.25mm (US3) needles, cast on 24 [24, 31] sts and work 8 rows [k1, p1] rib.
Change to 3.75mm (US5) needles and work in zigzag patt as for back until work measures 6 [7.5, 7.5]cm/2½ [3, 3]in, ending with a WS row.

Shape armhole
Next row (RS): Cast (bind) off 2 sts at beg of row, patt to end. *(22 [22, 29] sts)*
Next row: Purl.
Next row: Cast (bind) off 2 sts at beg of row, patt to end. *(20 [20, 27] sts)*
Dec 1 st at beg of foll alt row, patt to end. *(19 [19, 26] sts)*
Cont until armhole measures 4 [5, 5]cm/1½ [2, 2]in, ending with WS row (for left front; end with RS row for right front).
Next row (RS): Patt to last 9 [9, 11] sts, k2tog, turn. *11 [11, 16] sts*
(Leave 7, [7, 9] sts unworked. Leave these sts on a holder.)
Dec 1 st at same (neck) edge of next 3 [3, 5] rows, and for biggest size only on foll alt row. *(8 [8, 10] sts)*
Work without further shaping to same length as back shoulder.

Shape shoulder
Cast (bind) off 4 [4, 5] sts at beg next and foll alt row.

Right front
Work as left front, reversing shaping for armhole and neck.

Neckband

Join shoulder seams.

Using 3.25mm (US3) needles, knit 7 [7, 9] sts of right front neck sts from holder; pick up and knit 11 [11, 17] sts up right front neck, knit across 19, [22, 23] of back, pick up and knit 11 [11, 17] sts down left front neck and 7 [9, 9] from left front holder. *(55 [58, 75] sts)*
Work 4 rows garter st.
Cast (bind) off.

Right front band

Using 3.25mm (US3) needles, pick up and knit 24 [26, 33] sts (approx 3 sts for every 4 rows) from right front edge.
Knit 2 [5, 2] rows.
Next row (buttonhole row): K2 [3, 2], [yo, k2tog, k7] twice [twice, 3 times], yo, k2tog, k2 [3, 2].
Knit 2 [5, 2] rows.
Cast (bind) off.

Left front band

As right front, omitting buttonholes.

Sleeves (make 2)

Using 2.75mm (US2) needles, cast on 38 [45, 45] sts and work 6 rows [k1, p1] rib. Change to 3.75mm (US5) needles and work 8 rows in zigzag patt.

Shape cap

Cast (bind) off 2 [3, 2] sts at beg next 2 rows. *(34 [39, 41] sts)*
Dec 1 st at each end of every alt row until 16 [15, 15] sts rem.
Cast (bind) off loosely.

Finishing

Set in sleeves, then sew up side and sleeve seams.
Sew 3 [3, 4] buttons onto left front button band.
Block or press carefully as given on page 142.

ZIGZAG PATTERN CHART

KEY

	RS: knit / WS: purl
O	RS: yo / WS: yo
	RS: k2tog / WS: p2tog
	RS: ssk / WS: p2tog tbl
	repeat

'Foxglove' Zigzag Dress & Bolero

SIZE
To fit 6–9 [9–12, 12–18] months

FINISHED MEASUREMENTS
Dress: Chest 42 [48, 53]cm/17 [19, 21]in
Length (to back neck) 38 [43, 46]cm/15 [17, 18]in
Bloomers: Length 18cm/7in **Hips** 30cm/12in (one size)

MATERIALS
Yarn Sublime Baby Cashmere Merino Silk DK (75% extra fine merino wool, 20% silk, 5% cashmere, 116m/127yd): 8 [8, 9] x 50g/1¾oz balls shade Gooseberry 004
Needles 1 pair needles size 4mm (US6), 1 pair needles size 3.25mm (US3)
Notions 8 buttons, 1cm/⅜in diameter; 1.5m/59in ribbon, approx1cm/⅜in wide; 47cm/18in elastic, 12mm/½in wide

TENSION (GAUGE)
22 sts and 28 rows measure 10cm/4in over St st on 4mm (US6) needles (or size needed to obtain given tension/gauge)

'Meadowsweet' Dress & Bloomers

This pretty dress is typical of those worn in Queen Victoria's reign and beyond. The style, with puff sleeves and a full skirt falling from a yoke, was worn by boys and girls. It is a fashion that never dates and little girls seem to love wearing dresses like this. Until around 1920 girls would wear several layers of underwear beneath their dresses, with long bloomers that came down to the knees. To go with this dress, I have adapted a pattern for a pair of matching bloomers with the pretty lace pattern around the legs. Knitted in a mix of merino wool, silk and cashmere, this outfit will be soft and comfortable to wear every day or for a party.

DRESS
Front
Using 4mm (US6) needles, cast on 93 [108, 123] sts.
Row 1: K2, *yo, k5, ssk, k2tog, k5, yo, k1; rep from * 6 [7, 8] times to last st, k1.

Row 2 and all alt rows: Purl.
Rep these 2 rows until work measures 24 [27, 28]cm/9½ [10½, 11]in.
Next row: K1 [0, 1], k2tog to end. *(47 [54, 62] sts)*
Next row: Purl.

Make eyelets for ribbon
Next row (RS): K2, *yo, k2tog, k1; rep from * to last 0 [1, 0] sts, k0 [1, 0].
Next row: Purl.
Next 2 rows: Knit.

Begin yoke pattern
Row 1: Knit.
Row 2: Purl.
Row 3: Knit.
Row 4: Purl.
Row 5: Knit.
Row 6: Knit.

Shape armhole
Cast (bind) off 2 sts at beg of next 2 rows. *(43 [50, 58] sts)*
Dec 1 st at each end of next and every foll alt row until 37 [44, 52] sts rem.
Cont in yoke patt to approx 10 [11, 12]cm/4 [4½, 5]in from eyelet holes, ending after a row 1.

Shape neck
Row 1 (WS): P9 [11, 13], k19 [22, 26], p9 [11, 13].
Row 2 (RS): Knit.
Rep last 2 rows once more.
Next row (WS): K12 [15, 17], cast (bind) off 13 [14, 18] sts, k to end.
Work in yoke patt on last set of 12 [15, 17] sts, keeping 3 [4, 4] sts at neck edge in garter st.
When work measures 38 [43, 46]cm/ 15 [17, 18]in from hem, cast (bind) off. Rejoin yarn to rem 12 [15, 17] sts and work to match the other side.
Cast (bind) off.

Back
As front until eyelet holes have been made.
Next row: Purl.
Knit 2 rows.

Divide for back opening
Row 1 (RS): K26 [29, 33], turn.
Row 2: K4, p to end.
Row 3: Knit.
Rep the last 2 rows once more.
Row 6: Knit.

Shape armholes and make buttonholes
Row 1 (buttonhole row): Cast (bind) off 2 sts at beg of row, knit to last 3 sts, yo, k2tog, k1. *(24 [27, 31] sts)*
Row 2: K4, p to end.
Row 3: K2tog, k to end. *(23 [26, 30] sts)*
Row 4: K4, p to end.
Row 5: Knit.
Row 6 (buttonhole row): K1, k2tog, yo, k to end.
Row 7: K2tog, k to end. *(22 [25, 29] sts)*
Row 8: K4, p to end.
Cont in patt without further shaping, making buttonholes on 11th and every foll 5th row until work measures same as front to shoulder.
Cast (bind) off.

Return to rem 21 [25, 29] sts.
With RS facing, cast on 4 sts at beg of row and work to match first side, keeping the 4 edge sts in garter st but omitting buttonholes.
Cast (bind) off.

Sleeves (make 2)
Using 4mm (US6) needles, cast on 32 [40, 44] sts and knit 5 rows.
Next row (WS): K1, kfb in every st to last st, k1. *(62 [78, 86] sts)*
Work in yoke patt for 5 [6, 7]cm/ 2 [2½, 2¾]in.

Shape top
Cast (bind) off 2 sts at beg of next 2 rows. *(58 [74, 82] sts)*
Next row: Dec 1 st at each end of next and every alt row for 14 [16, 18] rows. *(44 [58, 64] sts)*
Without further shaping work 4 rows in patt.
Next row (dec row): [K2tog] to end. *(22 [29, 32] sts)*
Cast (bind) off.

Finishing
Join at shoulders.
Set in sleeves, then sew up side and sleeve seams.
Sew bottom edges of button band to inside of waist edge with a few stitches.
Sew on buttons.
Weave in ends.
Block or press carefully as given on page 142.
Thread ribbon through eyelets at waist.

BLOOMERS
Front
Lace trim (make 2 pieces the same)
Using 4mm (US6) needles, cast on 35 sts.
Purl 1 row.
Row 1: K3, *yo, k5, ssk, k2tog, k5, yo, k1; rep from * to last 2 sts, k2.
Row 2 and alt rows: Purl.
Rep these 2 rows 4 times more, then row 1 once more.
Next row (WS): K1, k2tog, k10, k2tog, k to last 3 sts, ssk, k1. *(32 sts)*
Knit 2 rows, break off yarn and leave sts on a holder.
Make a second piece the same but do not break off yarn.
Join pieces together to form front:
Row 1 (RS): K32, cast on 12, k32 from holder.
Row 2 and alt rows: Purl.
Row 3: K30, ssk, k12, k2tog, k30.
Row 5: K30, ssk, k10, k2tog, k30.
Cont dec in this way until
Row 17: K30, k2tog, k30. *(61 sts)*
Cont without shaping in St st to 9cm/ 3½in from cast-on sts at crotch.
Dec 1 st at each end of next and every foll 6th row until 55 sts rem.
Cont until work measures 14cm/5½in.
Change to 3.25mm (US3) needles and work in [k1, p1] rib for 3 rows.

Make eyelet holes

Next row: Rib 2, *yo, k2tog, p1, k1; rep from * to last st, k1.

Cont in rib for 4 more rows.

Cast (bind) off.

Back

As front until work measures 14cm/5½in.

Shape back (short rows)

Row 1: K49, w & t.

Row 2: P43, w & t.

Row 3: K37, w & t.

Row 4: P31, w & t.

Cont working 6 sts less each time until p7 (row 8) has been worked, w & t.

Next row (RS): Knit to end, picking up and knitting the wraps with their stitch as you go.

Next row: Purl all sts, again picking up the wraps as you go.

Change to 3.25mm (US3) needles and work 8 rows in [k1, p1] rib as for front, making eyelets on row 4.

Cast (bind) off.

Finishing

Join side seams, leaving side of lace section open.

Join crotch seam.

Weave in ends.

Block or press carefully as given on page 142.

Thread elastic through eyelet holes and stitch ends together.

'Wrap up Warm'

Cosy coats, hats and mittens

In the early half of the twentieth century children's outdoor wear was much more tailored than it is now. Coats and hats were knitted in stitches, such as moss (seed) stitch, that looked more like fabric than knitting. The items were utilitarian, rather than decorative like the matinée sets. The three patterns in this chapter are typical of the style that persisted until the 1950s and has since become fashionable again.

These patterns are timeless – the duffle coat and mittens (see opposite and page 124), in particular, could have been designed yesterday.

SIZE
To fit 6–9 [9–12] months

FINISHED MEASUREMENTS
Coat: Chest 43 [48]cm/17 [19]in **Length (to back neck)** 41 [43]cm/
16 [17]in **Sleeves** 16.5 [19]cm/6½ [7½]in
Beret: Crown to brim 22cm/8½in **Circumference** 40cm/16in

MATERIALS
Yarn Sublime Baby Cashmerino Silk DK (75% extra fine merino wool,
20% silk, 5% cashmere, 116m/127yd): 5 [6] x 50g/1¾oz balls shade Nutkin
Needles 1 pair 4mm (US6) needles, 1 pair 3.25mm (US3) needles, 4mm
(US6) and 3.25mm (US3) dpns or circular needle for magic loop method
(for beret)
Notions 4 buttons, 1.5cm/⅝in diameter

TENSION (GAUGE)
22 sts and 32 rows measure 10cm/4in over pattern on 4mm (US6) needles
(or size needed to obtain given tension/gauge)

'Betony' Coat & Beret

Over the course of the twentieth century children's clothing increasingly
began to resemble that of adults. It is difficult to date this design exactly,
as I only had a page of illustrations with no instructions or date. However,
comparing it to other items of a similar style suggests that it dates from the
early 1900s. This version is knitted in the softest blend of cashmere, silk and
lambswool to keep the baby warm and smart on a chilly day. The simple stitch
pattern is reminiscent of the tweed coats that babies often wore when they
were taken out in the pram (buggy) by their nannies.

COAT
Left front
Using 4mm (US6) needles, cast on
38 [44] sts.
Knit 1 row.

Begin pattern
Row 1: K5, *yo, ssk, k4; rep from *
to last 3 sts, yo, ssk, k1.
Row 2: K2, *p1, k5; rep from * to end.
Row 3: Knit.
Rep rows 2 and 3 once more, then
row 2 again.
Row 7: K2, *yo, ssk, k4; rep from *
to end.
Row 8: *K5, p1; rep from * to last

2 sts, k2.
Row 9: Knit.
Rep rows 8 and 9 once more, then
row 8 again.
These 12 rows form the patt.
Cont in patt until work measures
20 [21.5]cm/8 [8½]in, ending after
a 12th [6th] row.

Dec row (RS): K1 [4], *k2tog, k1; rep from * 12 times, k1 [4]. *(26 [32] sts)*

Work ribbed waist

Row 1 (WS): K2, *p1, k1; rep from * to end.

Row 2 (RS): *P1, k1; rep from * to end.

Row 3: Rep row 1.

Row 4 (eyelet row) (RS): K2, *yo, k2tog, p1, k1; rep from * to end (last 2 sts, k2).

Cont in rib for 3 more rows.

Yoke

Row 1: K5, *yo, ssk, k4; rep from * to last 3 sts, k3.

Row 2: K8, *p1, k5; rep from * to end.

Row 3: Knit.

Rep rows 2 and 3 once more, then row 2 again.

Row 7: K2, *yo, ssk, k4; rep from * to end.

Row 8: *K5, p1; rep from * to last 2 sts, k2.

Row 9: Knit.

Rep rows 8 and 9 once more, then row 8 again.

Shape armhole

Cast (bind) off 2 at beg of next row; k3, *yo, ssk, k4; rep from * to last 3 sts, k3. *(24 [30] sts)*

Next row (WS): K8, p1, *k5, p1; rep from * to last 3 sts, k3.

Next row (RS): K1, ssk, k to end. *(23 [29] sts)*

Next row: Patt to end.

Rep these 2 rows until 22 [26] sts rem. Cont in patt without further shaping until work measures 7 [9]cm/2¾ [3½]in from start of armhole, ending with a RS row.

Shape neck

Next row (WS): Cast (bind) off 2 sts at beg of row, work 5 [7] sts and leave them on a holder. *(15 [17] sts)*

Cont in patt as set, dec 1 st at neck edge on every row to 11 [12] sts. Cont without shaping until armhole measures 11.5 [13.5]cm/4½ [5]in, ending with a WS row.

Next row: Cast (bind) off 5 [6] sts at beg of row and 6 [6] sts on foll alt row.

Right front

Using 4mm (US6) needles, cast on 38 [44] sts.

Knit 1 row.

Begin pattern

Row 1: K2, *yo, ssk, k4; rep from * to end.

Row 2: *K5, p1; rep from * to last 2 sts, k2.

Row 3: Knit.

Rep rows 2 and 3 once more, then row 2 again.

Row 7: K5, *yo, ssk, k4; rep from * to last 3 sts, yo, ssk, k1.

Row 8: K2, *p1, k5; rep from * to end.

Row 9: Knit.

Rep rows 8 and 9 once more, then row 8 again.

Cont in patt until work measures 20 [21.5]cm/8 [8½]in, ending after a 12th [6th] row.

Dec row (RS): K1 [4], *K2tog, k1; rep from * 12 times, k1 [4]. *(26 [32] sts)*

Work ribbed waist

Row 1 (WS): P1, k1; rep from * to last 2 sts, k2.

Rep rib row twice more.

Make eyelets (RS): K2, *yo, k2tog, p1, k1; rep from * to end (last 2 sts, k2). Cont in rib for 3 more rows.

Yoke

Row 1: K8, *yo, ssk, k4; rep from *to end.

Row 2: *K5, p1; rep from * to last 8 sts, k8.

Row 3: Knit.

Row 4: As row 2.

Row 5 (make buttonhole): K2, yo, k2tog, k to end.

Cont as for left front reversing armhole and neck shaping, making a buttonhole on every 10th row.

Back

Using 4mm (US6) needles cast on 65 (71) sts.

Knit 1 row.

Begin pattern

Row 1: K2, *yo, ssk, k4; rep from * to last 3 sts, yo, ssk, k1.

Row 2: K2, *p1, k5; rep from * to last 3 sts, p1, k2.

Row 3: Knit.

Rep rows 2 and 3 once more, then row 2 again.

Row 7: K5, *yo, ssk, k4; rep from * to end.

Row 8: K5, *p1, k5; rep from * to end.

Row 9: Knit.

Rep rows 8 and 9 once more, then row 8 again.

Cont in patt until work measures 20 [21.5]cm/8 [8½]in, ending after a 12th [6th] row.

Dec row (RS): K2 [4], *k2tog, k1; rep from * 21 times, k0 [4]. *(44 [50] sts)*

Work ribbed waist

Row 1 (WS): K2, *p1, k1; rep from * to end.

Row 2 (RS): *P1, k1; rep from * to end.

Row 3: Rep row 1.

Row 4 (eyelet row): K2, *yo, k2tog, p1, k1; rep from * to last 2 [0] sts, yo, k2tog [0].

Cont in rib for 3 more rows.

Inc row: K2, yo, k5, [yo, ssk, k4] twice, [yo, k5] twice, [yo, ssk, k4] twice [3 times], yo, ssk, k1. *(47 [53] sts)*

Cont in patt from row 2 until work measures same as fronts to armholes, ending with a WS row.

Shape armholes
Keeping patt correct, cast (bind) off 2 sts at beg of next 2 rows. *(43 [49] sts)* Dec 1 st at each end of next and foll alt row to 39 [45] sts.
Cont in patt without further shaping until armhole measures the same as fronts to shoulder shaping.

Shape shoulders
Cast (bind) off 5 [6] sts at beg of next 2 rows and 6 [6] sts at beg of foll 2 rows.
Leave rem 17 [21] sts on a holder or length of scrap yarn.
Join shoulder seams.

Collar
With RS facing, knit 5 [7] sts from RF holder onto 3.25mm (US3) needle, pick up and knit 15 [17] sts up RF neck, knit 17 [21] sts from back holder, pick up and knit 15 [17] sts down LF neck, and knit 5 [7] sts from LF holder. *(57 [69] sts)* Work 4 rows garter st (knit every row) inc 1 st at each end of next row. *(59 [71] sts)*
Next row: Knit.
Change to 4mm (US6) needles and work 2 rows garter st.
Next row: Inc 1 st at each end of row. *(61 [73] sts)*
Cont in garter st until collar measures 6cm [2¼]in.
Cast (bind) off loosely.

Sleeves (make 2)
Using 4mm (US6) needles, cast on 26 [26] sts.
Knit 1 row.
Work 12 rows in patt as for LF.
Knit 1 row.
Work 8 rows [k1, p1] rib.

Cont in patt, inc 1 st at each end of every 6th row to 40 [44] sts.
Cont until sleeve measures 16.5 [19]cm/ 6½ [7½]in with cuff turned back at beg of rib rows.

Shape cap
Keeping patt correct, dec 1 st at each end of next and every alt row until 14 sts rem.
Cast (bind) off loosely.

Finishing
Set in sleeves. Join side and sleeve seams.
Sew on buttons.
Weave in all ends.
Block or press carefully as given on page 142.
Make a twisted or crochet cord approx 61cm/24in long and thread through holes at waist. Make two tassels and attach to ends of cord.

BERET
Using size 4mm (US6) dpns or circular needle, cast on 10 sts.
Join to work in the round, being careful not to twist sts.
Knit 1 round.
Round 2: Kfb in every stitch. *(20 sts)*
Round 3: Knit.
Round 4: [M1R, k1, m1L, k3] 5 times. *(30 sts)*
Round 5: Knit.
Round 6: K1, [m1R, k1, m1L, k5] 4 times to last 5 sts, m1R, k1, m1L, k4. *(40 sts)*
Round 7: Knit.
Round 8: K2, [m1R, k1, m1L, k7] 4 times to last 6 sts, m1R, k1, m1L, k5. *(50 sts)*
Round 9: Knit.
Cont inc on alt rnds in this way, each side of knit st to 120 sts.

Work in pattern as for coat
Round 1: *K4, yo, k2tog; rep from

* to end.
Round 2: *P4, k1, p1; rep from * to end.
Round 3: Knit.
Round 4: As round 2.
Round 5: As round 3.
Round 6: As round 2.
Round 7: K1, *yo, k2tog, k4; rep from * to last 5 sts, yo, k2tog, k3.
Round 8: *P1, k1, p4; rep from * to end.
Cont in patt as set for 5cm/2in.
Next round (dec rnd): *K4, k2tog; rep from * to end. *(100 sts)*
Change to 3.25mm (US3) needles and work [k1, p1] rib for 4cm/1½in.
Cast (bind) off loosely.

Finishing
Weave in ends.
Make a short cord and tassel, as for coat, and attach to centre of beret.

SIZE
To fit 6–9 [9–12, 12–18] months
To fit chest 41 [46, 51]cm/16 [18, 20]in

FINISHED MEASUREMENTS
Jacket: Actual chest size 46 [51, 56]cm/18 [20, 22]in **Length (to back neck)** 33 [36, 40]cm/13 [14, 15½]in **Sleeves** 15 [19, 21.5]cm/6 [7½, 8½]in
Hat: Crown to brim 18cm/7in **Circumference** 40cm/16in (one size)

MATERIALS
Yarn Shilasdair Luxury DK (10% cashmere, 10% baby camel, 40% angora, 40% merino lambswool, 302m/330yd): 2 [2, 3] x 100g/3½oz balls shade Juniper (MC), 1 [1, 1] x 100g/3½oz ball (small amount needed) shade Natural (CC)
Needles 1 pair needles size 4mm (US6), 1 pair needles size 3.75mm (US5), 1 pair needles size 3.25mm (US3), 2 stitch holders
Notions 6 [6, 7] buttons, 1.5cm/⅝in diameter

TENSION (GAUGE)
20 sts and 32 rows measure 10cm/4in over moss (seed) stitch on 4mm (US6) needles (or size needed to obtain given tension/gauge)

'Stitchwort' Jacket & Bobble Hat

This cute jacket is knitted in a moss (seed) stitch to imitate tweed fabric. The design probably dates from the early decades of the nineteenth century. I had no pattern instructions, so I designed it in a mix of cashmere and lambswool to be warm enough for the chilliest of days. The jacket buttons high at the neck, but this yarn will be soft on the baby's skin. It is knitted in a simple moss-stitch (seed-stitch) pattern, but some unusual buttons, such as these vintage figurative ones, will instantly make it more decorative. Remember to place the buttonholes on the left side for a boy and on the right side for a girl. The brim of the hat can be folded up or down to keep the ears warm.

Moss-stitch (seed-stitch) pattern
(Over even number of sts.)
Row 1: *K1, p1; rep from * to end.
Row 2: *P1, k1; rep from * to end.

JACKET
Body
(Worked in one piece to armholes, bottom up.)
Using size 4mm (US6) needles and MC, cast on 100 [112, 122] sts and knit 12 rows.

Cont in moss (seed) stitch, making [yo, k2tog] buttonholes 3 sts from end, on first and every foll 18th [19th, 18th]

row. (Make them at beg of row for a girl and at the end for a boy.) When work measures 21.5 [23, 25.5]cm/8½ [9, 10]in divide for fronts and back, cont to work buttonholes as before:

Next row: Moss (seed) st 25 [28, 31] sts, cast (bind) off 2 sts, moss (seed) st 46 [52, 56] sts, cast (bind) off 2 sts, moss (seed) st 25 [28, 31] sts. Cont on last set of sts, which will be the left front.

Work in moss (seed) st until armhole measures 11 [13, 14]cm/4½ [5, 5½]in. Break yarn and leave these 25 [28, 31] sts on a holder.

Back

With WS facing, rejoin yarn to centre 46 [52, 56] sts and work to same length as front.
Break yarn and leave sts on a holder.

Right front

With WS facing, rejoin yarn to rem sts and work to match left front, ending at the armhole edge.
Do not break yarn.
Turn work inside out and, holding sts of RF and back together, join by casting (binding) off 13 [14, 15] sts of shoulder tog with those of back (3-needle cast-off/bind-off), moss (seed) st 20 [24, 26] sts across back, then cast (bind) off the left shoulder sts in the same way. Break yarn, draw through rem st and fasten off.

Collar

With RS facing, rejoin MC yarn to RF

at collar, moss (seed) st 12 [14, 16] sts, moss (seed) st 20 [24, 26] sts across back, moss (seed) st 12 [14, 16] sts of LF collar. *(44 [52, 58] sts)*
Work in moss (seed) st for 6cm/2½in, ending with inside of collar facing.
Break MC yarn.

Next row: Change to CC and knit 7 rows.
Cast (bind) off loosely.

Sleeves (make 2)

(Worked from the top down.)
Using 4mm (US6) needles and MC, cast on 45 [49, 55] sts and work 12.5 [16.5, 19]cm/5 [6½, 7½]in in moss (seed) st.
Dec 1 st at end of last row.

Next row: Change to 3.75mm (US5) needles and work 7 rows [k2, p2] rib.

Next row: With WS facing, change to CC and knit 9 rows.
Cast (bind) off.

Finishing

Set in sleeves, then sew up sleeve seams so that CC cuff folds back to right side.
Sew on buttons.
Weave in all ends.
Block or press carefully as given on page 142.

HAT

Using 3.25mm (US3) needles and CC, cast on 85 sts and knit 13 rows, dec 1 st at end of last row. *(84 sts)*
Break CC yarn.
Change to 3.75mm (US5) needles and,

using MC, knit 1 row.
Work 11cm/4¼in moss (seed) st, ending with RS facing.
(The CC brim will fold up at the end, so be careful to start decreases on correct side.)

Shape top
Row 1: K5, [k2tog, k10] 6 times, k2tog, k5. *(77 sts)*
Row 2 and all alt rows until stated otherwise: Purl.
Row 3: K4, [k2tog, k9] 6 times, k2tog, k5. *(70 sts)*
Row 5: K3, [k2tog, k8] 6 times, k2tog, k5. *(63 sts)*
Row 7: K2, [k2tog, k7] 6 times, k2tog, k5. *(56 sts)*
Row 9: K1, [k2tog, k6] 6 times, k2tog, k5. *(49 sts)*
Row 10: [P5, p2tog] to end. *(44 sts)*
Row 11: K5, [k2tog, k4] 5 times, k2tog, k5. *(36 sts)*
Row 12: [P2tog, p3] to last st, k1. *(29 sts)*
Row 13: K3, [k2tog, k2] 6 times, k1. *(22 sts)*
Row 14: [P2tog, p1] 7 times, p1. *(15 sts)*
Row 15: K1, [k2tog] 7 times. *(8 sts)*
Break yarn, thread through rem 8 sts, draw up and fasten off.

Finishing

Join back seam. Before breaking yarn fold back contrast edging to right side and stitch in place at seam.
Make pompom in CC and sew to top of hat.
Weave in ends.

SIZE
To fit 12–18 [18–24] months
To fit chest 46 [51]cm/18 [20]in

FINISHED MEASUREMENTS
Coat: Actual chest size 51 [56]cm/20 [22]in **Length (to back neck)** 38 [43]cm/15 [17]in
Sleeves 19 [21.5]cm/7½ [8½]in
Mittens: Length 20cm/8in **Circumference** 15cm/6in

MATERIALS
Yarn Brown Sheep Nature Spun Sport Weight (100% wool, 168m/184yd):
4 [5] x 50g/1¾oz balls shade 200 Bordeaux
Needles 1 pair needles size 3.75mm (US5), 1 pair needles size 3mm (US2–3),
1 stitch holder, 2 safety pins (for mittens)
Notions 6 small toggle buttons, 3.5cm/1½in long; 1 button, 1cm/⅜in diameter, 1 small snap fastener

TENSION (GAUGE)
24 sts and 36 rows measure 10cm/4in over St st on 3.75mm (US5) needles
(or size needed to obtain given tension/gauge)

'Poppy' Duffle Coat & Mittens

A warm, woolly coat is essential for playing outside when the weather turns cooler, and this one is even cosier with its matching mittens. With its double-breasted design and attractive toggle buttons, it is also smart enough for going visiting. Children's coats were knitted to look very much like their fabric counterparts and styles for boys and girls were similar, invariably double-breasted and often with a half belt at the back. Mittens were usually joined together with a long, twisted cord made from the same yarn; the cord was threaded up one sleeve of the coat, around the back of the neck and down through the other sleeve, to prevent the child from losing one or both mittens.

COAT
Right front
Using 3.75mm (US5) needles, cast on 47 [56] sts and knit 5 rows.

Begin pattern
Row 1 (WS): K1 [p7, k2] 4 [5] times, p7, k3.
Row 2: Knit.
Rep these 2 rows 4 times more, then row 1 again.
Row 12 (RS): K to last 3 sts, k2tog, k1. (46 [55] sts)
Knit 4 rows.
Row 17: K1, p6, [k2, p7] to last 3 sts, k3.

Row 18: Knit.

Rep rows 17 and 18 twice more, then row 17 again.

Row 24: K to last 3 sts, k2tog, k1. *(45 [54] sts)*

Row 25: K1, p5, [k2, p7] to last 3 sts, k3.

Row 26: Knit.

Rep last 2 rows once more.

Knit 4 rows.

Rows 33 and 35: As row 25.

Row 34: Knit.

Row 36: K to last 3 sts, k2tog, k1. *(44 [53] sts)*

Row 37: K1, p4, [k2, p7] to last 3 sts, k3.

Row 38: Knit.

Rep last 2 rows 3 times more.

Knit 3 rows.

Row 48: K to last 3 sts, k2tog, k1. *(43 [52] sts)*

Row 49: K1, p21 [30], [k2, p7] twice, k3.

Row 50: Knit.

Rep last 2 rows 4 times more, then row 49 again.

Row 60: K to last 3 sts, k2tog, k1. *(42 [51] sts)*

Row 61: K1, p20 [29], k21.

Row 62: Knit.

Rep last 2 rows once more.

Row 65: K1, p20 [29], [k2, p7] twice, k3.

Row 66: Knit.

Rep last 2 rows 5 times more.

(For second size only, cont dec every 12th row as before until 47 sts rem.)

Row 77: As row 61.

Row 78: Knit.

Rep the last 2 rows once more.

Rep patt from row 65 until the side

edge measures 26 [30]cm/10 [12]in, ending with a RS row.

Shape armhole

Next row (WS): Cast (bind) off 3 [4] sts at beg of row, patt to end. *(39 [43] sts)*

Dec 1 st at armhole edge on next and foll 3 alt rows. *(35 [39] sts)*

Cont until armhole measures 7 [8]cm/ 2¾ [3]in, ending with a RS row.

Next row (buttonhole row) (WS): Patt to last 4 sts, k2tog, yo, k2.

Work 2 rows in patt.

Next row (RS): Cast (bind) off 17 sts, k to end. *(18 [22] sts)*

Dec 1 st at neck edge on next 5 [8] rows. *(13 [14] sts)*

Cont without shaping until armhole measures 11.5 [12]cm/4½ [4¾]in, ending with a RS row.

Shape shoulder

Next row (WS): Cast (bind) off 7 [7] sts at beg of next row and 6 [7] sts at beg of foll alt row.

Left front

As right front, reversing shaping and position of squares.

Back

Using 3.75mm (US5) needles, cast on 70 [88] sts and knit 5 rows.

Begin pattern

Row 1 (WS): P7, [k2, p7] to end.

Row 2: Knit.

Rep these 2 rows 4 times more,

then row 1 again.

Row 12: K1, ssk, k to last 3 sts, k2tog, k1. *(68 [86] sts)*

Knit 4 rows.

Row 17: P6, [k2, p7] to last 8 sts, k2, p6.

Cont in patt as for right front, dec at each end of every 12th row.

When row 47 has been completed, cont in St st until 60 [72] sts rem.

Cont without shaping until back measures same as fronts to armhole, ending with a WS row.

Shape armholes

Cast (bind) off 3 [4] sts at beg of next 2 rows. *(54 [64] sts)*

Dec 1 st at each end of next and foll 3 alt rows. *(46 [56] sts)*

Cont until armhole measures 11.5 [12]cm/4½ [4¾]in, ending with a WS row.

Shape shoulders

Cast (bind) off 7 [7] sts at beg of next 2 rows and 6 [7] sts at beg of foll 2 rows. *(20 [28] sts)*

Break yarn and leave these sts on a holder.

Sleeves (make 2)

Using 3mm (US2–3) needles, cast on 44 sts and work 10 rows garter st (knit every row).

Change to 3.75mm (US5) needles and cont in St st, inc 1 st at each of 7th and every foll 6th row to 54 [60] sts.

Cont without further shaping until sleeve measures 19 [21.5]cm/7½ [8½]in, ending with a WS row.

Shape top

Next row (RS): Cast (bind) off 3 sts at beg of next 2 rows. *(48 [54] sts)*

Dec 1 st at each end of every alt row until 24 [30] sts rem.

Dec 1 st at each end every row until 16 [20] sts rem.

Cast (bind) off.

Join shoulder seams.

Collar

Using 3mm (US2–3) needles, with RS facing, and beg 12 sts in from right front edge, pick up and knit 5 sts from cast-off (bound-off) sts, 16 [18] sts from neck edge, 20 [28] sts from back neck, 16 [18] sts down left front neck, and 5 sts from cast-off (bound-off) sts. *(62 [74] sts)*

Work 5 rows [k1, p1] rib.

Change to 3.75mm (US5) needles and work 10 rows more in rib.

Cast (bind) off loosely.

Finishing

Set in sleeves, then sew up side and sleeve seams.

Block or press carefully as given on page 142.

Make buttonhole loops at end of rows with garter-st ridges (on right or left front, depending on whether coat is for a boy or a girl). Sew toggles to inner end of same rows. Sew toggles to inner end of opposite front. Sew button at neck. Sew snap fastener to inside neck edge just below collar, closing up buttonhole where not required.

MITTENS (MAKE 2)

Using 3mm (US2–3) needles, cast on 40 sts and work 12 rows [k1, p1] rib. Change to 3.75mm (US5) needles and beg with a k row, work 3cm/1¼in St st.

Next row (RS): K16, slip next 8 sts onto a safety pin for thumb, k to end. *(32 sts)*

Cont in St st to 12cm/4¾in.

Shape top

Row 1: *K2, k2tog; rep from * to end. *(24 sts)*

Next row: Purl.

Next row: K2tog to end. *(12 sts)* Break yarn and thread through rem sts, draw up and fasten off.

Thumb

With RS facing, pick up and knit 2 sts before safety pin, knit 8 sts from safety pin, and pick up and knit 2 sts after safety pin. *(12 sts)*

Work 11 rows St st.

Next row (RS): K2tog to end. *(6 sts)* Break yarn and thread through rem sts, draw up and fasten off.

Finishing

Join side seam and thumb seam.

Weave in all ends.

'Poppy' Duffle Coat & Mittens

'Knitted Friends'

Adorable soft toys for little ones

Knitted toys were often designed to be made by children themselves. Many girls had learnt to knit by the time they were five years old, and they were encouraged to make things for their baby brothers and sisters. Consequently, manufacturers produced patterns that were not too difficult, often in plain garter stitch, as is this cat toy (see opposite and page 136). During the Second World War toy production virtually stopped, so more people made toys at home and knitting patterns for toys became prolific. The animal patterns in this chapter are typical of those produced just after the war; the bricks are my own design, imitating the wooden ones that virtually every child had.

FINISHED MEASUREMENTS
Height Approx 37cm/15in

MATERIALS
Yarn Artesano Aran (50% superfine alpaca, 50% Peruvian highland wool, 132m/144⅓yd): 2 x 100g/3½oz balls shade Fleet, plus oddments of DK (worsted) or Aran (fisherman) yarn in different colours for scarf
Needles 1 pair needles size 5mm (US8), 2 stitch holders or safety pins
Notions Toy-grade stuffing

TENSION (GAUGE)
Approx 17 sts and 21 rows measure 10cm/4in over St st on 5mm (US8) needles, although tension (gauge) is not too important for this project

'Bramble' Teddy Bear

Dolls in the form of animals have always been popular with babies and young children, and the teddy bear seems to be an eternal favourite. Unlike most of today's patterns for knitted toys, the early ones were very simple, with little or no shaping for the head and the limbs, but this one has a nicely shaped head and also hands and feet. The original design called for a large ribbon bow, but I have updated this teddy with a scarf around his neck; it provides a great opportunity to use up some of your stash to make it nice and colourful.

Head
Cast on 11 sts and work in St st throughout.
Row 1: Knit.
Row 2: Purl.
Next row (RS): Inc 1 st at each end of next and foll 2 alt rows. (*17 sts*) Work 11 rows.
Next row (RS): Dec 1 st at each end of next and foll 2 alt rows. (*11 sts*) Work 3 rows.
Next row (RS): Inc 1 st at each end of next and foll 3 alt rows. (*19 sts*) Work 5 rows.

Next row (RS): K14, slip rem 5 sts onto a safety pin, turn.
Next row: P9, slip rem 5 sts onto another safety pin, turn.
Next row (RS): Work 9 rows on rem 9 sts.
Cont on the RS, pick up and knit 5 sts along side of the 9 rows just knitted, k5 sts from safety pin. (*19 sts*)
Next row (WS): P19, pick up and purl 5 sts along other side and p5 sts from other safety pin. (*29 sts*)

Decrease for shaping
Row 1 (RS): K2tog, k10, k2tog, k1, ssk, k10, ssk. (*25 sts*)
Row 2: P10, p2tog, p1, p2tog, p10. (*23 sts*)
Row 3: K2tog, k7, k2tog, k1, ssk, k7, ssk. (*19 sts*)
Row 4: P7, p2tog, p1, p2tog, p7. (*17 sts*)
Row 5: K2tog, k4, k2tog, k1, ssk, k4, ssk. (*13 sts*)
Row 6: P2tog, p9, p2tog. (*11 sts*)
Cast (bind) off.

Body (make 2)

Cast on 3 sts and work 2 rows St st.

Next row (RS): Inc 1 st at each end of next and foll 7 alt rows. *(19 sts)*
Work 3 rows.

Next row: Inc 1 st at each end of next row. *(21 sts)*
Work 5 rows.

Next row: Dec 1 st at each end of next and foll 3 alt rows. *(13 sts)*

Next row: Dec 1 st at each end of next 2 rows. *(9 sts)*
Cast (bind) off.

Legs (make 2)

Cast on 15 sts and work 22 rows St st.

Next row: *K1, k2tog; rep from * to end. *(10 sts)*

Next row: P7, slip rem 3 sts onto a safety pin, turn.

Next row: K4, slip rem 3 sts onto another safety pin, turn.
Work 5 rows on these 4 sts.
Cont on the WS, pick up and purl 3 sts along side of the 5 rows just knitted, p3 from safety pin. *(10 sts)*

Next row: K10 then pick up and knit 3 sts down other side, k3 from second safety pin. *(16 sts)*
Work 3 rows St st.
Cast (bind) off.

Arms (make 2)

Cast on 14 sts and work 18 rows St st.

Next row: K2tog, k3, k2tog, ssk, k3, ssk. *(10 sts)*

Next row: Purl.

Next row: K2tog, k1, k2tog, ssk, k1, ssk. *(6 sts)*
Cast (bind) off.

Ears (make 4)

Cast on 5 sts and work 2 rows St st.
Inc 1 st at each end of next and foll alt row. *(9 sts)*
Work 3 rows.

Next row: K1, [k2tog] to end. *(6 sts)*
Cast (bind) off.

Finishing

Block or press carefully as given on page 142.
Join sides of neck and shoulder seams. Join two halves of body leaving approx 3cm/1¼in at top to insert arms.
Fold arms and legs in half and sew seams, leaving an opening to insert stuffing. Stuff firmly and close opening. Insert arms into armholes and sew in place. Finish stuffing body. Insert legs into holes at base of body and sew in place.
Sew fronts of ears to backs.
Fold head piece in half, placing cast-on edge to cast-off (bound-off) edge. Join side seams, inserting ears securely. Stuff firmly. Sew head to body. Embroider features. Eyes can be made by working a small circle of double (single) crochet, or they can be embroidered with chain stitch.

Scarf

Using 5mm (US8) needles, cast on 100 sts and work 13 rows garter st (knit every row) in stripes of 2 rows each colour. When joining in new colours, leave ends for fringe at one side.
Cast (bind) off.
Make fringe on the other side.

'Bramble' Teddy Bear

FINISHED MEASUREMENTS
Height Approx 30cm/12in

MATERIALS
Yarn Blacker Swan DK (100% wool, 109m/119yd): 1 x 50g/1¾oz ball shade Seafoam Blue (MC), 1 x 50g/1¾oz ball shade Teaberry Pink (CC), plus small amount of black yarn for eyes and nose, and small amount of white yarn for pompom tail

Needles 1 pair needles size 3.75mm (US5)

Notions Toy-grade stuffing

TENSION (GAUGE)
Not important for this project

'Primrose' Rabbit

Children's playthings in the early part of the twentieth century were often very simple. There were wooden toys, such as building bricks, block-shaped trains and rectangular toy soldiers, and every nursery had its quota of dolls and toy animals. They were usually made from scraps of fabric, but around 1940 knitted toys became popular. There were patterns for long-legged dolls and familiar animals, such as ducks, cats and rabbits. This bunny is made in two simple pieces, so there are no awkward arms and legs to sew on.

Back and sides of body
Using MC, cast on 75 sts.

Row 1 (WS): Purl.

Row 2: K1, KLL, k29, [KLL, k5] 3 times, KLL, k29, KLL, k1. (81 sts)

Rows 3–5: Work St st.

Row 6: K1, ssk, knit to last 3 sts, k2tog, k1. (79 sts)

Row 7: P1, p2tog, purl to last 3 sts, p2tog, p1. (77 sts)

Row 8: Cast (bind) off 12 sts, knit rem sts. (65 sts)

Row 9: Cast (bind) off 12 sts, purl rem sts. (53 sts)

Row 10: K1, ssk, knit to last 3 sts, k2tog, k1. (51 sts)

Rows 11–17: Work St st.

Row 18: K1, ssk, knit to last 3 sts, k2tog, k1. (49 sts)

Rows 19–34: Rep rows 11–18 twice more. (45 sts)

Cont in St st without further shaping until piece measures 12.5cm/5in from cast-on edge, finishing with a WS row.

Shape front legs
Row 1(RS): K1, KLL, knit to last st, KLL, k1. (47 sts)

Row 2: Cast on 8 sts, purl to end of row. (55 sts)

Row 3: Cast on 8 sts, knit to end of row. (63 sts)

Row 4: P1, PLL, purl to last st, PLL, p1. (65 sts)

Rows 5–9: Work St st.

Row 10: P1, p2tog, purl to last 3 sts, p2tog, p1. (63 sts)

Row 11: K1, ssk, knit to last 3 sts, k2tog, k1. (61 sts)

Row 12: Cast (bind) off 9 sts, purl rem sts. (52 sts)

Row 13: Cast (bind) off 9 sts, knit rem sts. (43 sts)

Row 14: P1, p2tog, purl to last 3 sts, p2tog, p1. (41 sts)

Row 15: K1, ssk, k13, k2tog, k5, ssk, k13, k2tog, k1. *(37 sts)*
Rows 16–18: Work St st.
Row 19: K1, ssk, k11, k2tog, k5, ssk, k11, k2tog, k1. *(33 sts)*
Rows 20–22: Work St st.
Row 23: K1, ssk, k9, k2tog, k5, ssk, k9, k2tog, k1. *(29 sts)*
Row 24: P14, p2tog, p13. *(28 sts)*

Shape sides of head
Row 1: K14, turn.
Row 2: P14 to end.

Work the foll 14 rows over these first 14 sts:
Row 1: Cast on 2 sts, knit to last st, KLL, k1. *(17 sts)*
Row 2: Purl to last st, PLL, p1. *(18 sts)*
Row 3: Cast on 2 sts, knit to end of row. *(20 sts)*
Rows 4–6: Work St st.
Row 7: Cast (bind) off 2 sts. Knit to last 2 sts, KLL, k1. *(19 sts)*
Row 8: Purl to last 3 sts, p2tog, p1. *(18 sts)*
Row 9: Cast (bind) off 2 sts, knit to end of row. *(16 sts)*
Row 10: Purl to last 3 sts, p2tog, p1. *(15 sts)*
Row 11: Cast (bind) off 2 sts, knit to end of row. *(13 sts)*
Row 12: P1, p2tog, purl to last 3 sts, p2tog, p1. *(11 sts)*
Row 13: Cast (bind) off 2 sts knit to last 3 sts, k2tog, k1. *(8 sts)*
Row 14: Cast (bind) off 2 sts, purl to last 3 sts, p2tog, p1. *(5 sts)*
Cast (bind) off rem sts.

With RS facing, return to rem 14 sts.
Rows 1–3: Work St st.
Row 4: Cast on 2 sts, purl to last st, PLL, p1. *(17 sts)*
Row 5: Knit to last st, KLL, k1. *(18 sts)*

Row 6: Cast on 2 sts, purl to end of row. *(20 sts)*
Rows 7–9: Work St st.
Row 10: Cast (bind) off 2 sts. Purl to last 2 sts, PLL, p1. *(19 sts)*
Row 11: Knit to last 3 sts, k2tog, k1. *(18 sts)*
Row 12: Cast (bind) off 2 sts, purl to end of row. *(16 sts)*
Row 13: Knit to last 3 sts, k2tog, k1. *(15 sts)*
Row 14: Cast (bind) off 2 sts, purl to end of row. *(13 sts)*
Row 15: K1, ssk, knit to last 3 sts, k2tog, k1. *(11 sts)*
Row 16: Cast (bind) off 2 sts purl to last 3 sts, p2tog, p1. *(8 sts)*
Row 17: Cast (bind) off 2 sts, knit to last 3 sts, k2tog, k1. *(5 sts)*
Cast (bind) off rem sts.

Top of head
Using MC, cast on 3 sts.

Row 1–3: Beg with a P row, work 3 rows St st.
Row 4 (RS): K1, KLL, knit to last st, KLL, k1. *(5 sts)*
Rows 5–12: Rep rows 1–4 twice more. *(9 sts)*
Row 13: Purl.
Row 14: K1, KLL, knit to last st, KLL, k1. *(11 sts)*
Rows 15–16: Rep rows 13–14. *(13 sts)*
Row 17–21: Work St st.
Row 22: K1, KLL, knit to last st, KLL, k1. *(15 sts)*
Rows 23–27: Work St st.
Row 28: K1, ssk, knit to last 3 sts, k2tog, k1. *(13 sts)*
Rows 29–31: Work St st.
Rows 32–47: Rep rows 28–31 4 more times. *(5 sts)*
Row 48: Ssk, k1, k2tog. *(3 sts)*
Row 49: K3tog. *(1 st)*

Break yarn, draw through rem st and fasten off.

Front of body
Using CC, cast on 46 sts.

Row 1 (WS): Purl.
Row 2: K1, KLL, knit to last st, KLL, k1. *(48 sts)*
Rows 3–5: Work St st.
Row 6: K1, ssk, knit to last 3 sts, k2tog, k1. *(46 sts)*
Row 7: P1, p2tog, purl to last 3 sts, p2tog, p1. *(44 sts)*
Row 8: Cast (bind) off 12 sts, knit to end of row. *(32 sts)*
Row 9: Cast (bind) off 12 sts, purl to end of row. *(20 sts)*
Row 10: K1, k2tog, knit to last 3 sts k2tog, k1. *(18 sts)*
Rows 11–17: Work 7 rows St st.
Row 18: K1, ssk, knit to last 3 sts k2tog, k1. *(16 sts)*
Rep last 8 rows until 12 sts rem.
Cont in St st without further shaping until piece measures 12.5cm/5in from cast-on edge, finishing with a WS row.

Shape front legs
Row 1: K1, KLL, knit until last st, KLL, k1. *(14 sts)*
Row 2: Cast on 8 sts, purl to end of row. *(22 sts)*
Row 3: Cast on 8 sts, knit to end of row. *(30 sts)*
Row 4: P1, PLL, purl to last st, PLL, p1. *(32 sts)*
Rows 5–9: Work St st.
Row 10: P1, p2tog, purl to last 3 sts, p2tog, p1. *(30 sts)*
Row 11: K1, ssk, knit to last 3 sts, k2tog, k1. *(28 sts)*
Row 12: Cast (bind) off 9 sts, purl rem sts. *(19 sts)*
Row 13: Cast (bind) off 9 sts, knit rem sts. *(10 sts)*

Row 14: P1, p2tog, purl to last 3 sts, p2tog, p1. *(8 sts)*

Rows 15–16: Work St st.

Row 17: K1, ssk, knit to last 3 sts, k2tog, k1. *(6 sts)*

Rows 18–19: Work St st.

Row 20: P1, p2tog, purl to last 3 sts, p2tog, p1. *(4 sts)*

Rows 21–22: Work St st.

Row 23: Ssk, k2tog. *(2 sts)*

Row 24: K2tog. *(1 st)*

Break yarn, draw through rem st and fasten off.

Ears (make 2)
Back

Using MC, cast on 14 sts.

Work 7cm/3in St st.

Next row: K4, k2tog, k2, ssk, k4. *(12 sts)*

Work 5 rows without shaping.

Cont dec in this way on every 6th row, either side of the centre 2 sts until 4 sts rem.

Next row: Purl.

Next row: K2tog, ssk. *(2 sts)*

Next row: P2tog.

Break yarn, draw through rem st and fasten off.

Front

Using CC, cast on 12 sts and work as for back.

Seat

Using MC, cast on 24 sts.

Row 1 (WS): Purl.

Row 2: K1, KLL, knit to last st, KLL, k1. *(26 sts)*

Row 3: Purl.

Row 4: K1, KLL, knit to end of row. *(27 sts)*

Row 5: Purl.

Row 6: K1, KLL, knit to end of row. *(28 sts)*

Row 7: Purl.

Row 8: Knit to last 3 sts, k2tog, k1. *(27 sts)*

Row 9: Cast (bind) off 12 sts, purl to end. *(15 sts)*

Row 10: K1, KLL, knit to last 3 sts, k2tog, k1. *(15 sts)*

Rows 11–22: Work St st.

Row 23: P1, PLL, purl to end of row. *(16 sts)*

Row 24: K1, ssk, knit to end of row. *(15 sts)*

Row 25: Cast on 12 sts, purl to end. *(27 sts)*

Row 26: Knit to last st, KLL, k1. *(28 sts)*

Row 27: Purl.

Row 28: K1, ssk, knit to end of row. *(27 sts)*

Row 29: Purl.

Row 30: K1, ssk, knit to end of row. *(26 sts)*

Row 31: Purl.

Row 32: K1, ssk, knit to last 3 sts, k2tog, k1. *(24 sts)*

Row 33: Purl.

Cast (bind) off all sts.

Finishing

Block or press the pieces carefully as given on page 142, if required.

Sew the top of head into position, placing the cast-on edge at the back of neck and the cast-off (bound-off) sts coming to the nose. Commencing at nose, sew the front into position until it is sewn up 1.5cm/½in below the front paws.

Stuff the head, neck and front paws. Sew the remainder of the front into position. Sew the leg part of the 'seat' into position and stuff.

Sew together front and back ear pieces and press, then fold the ears in half at lower edge and sew into position.

Using the black wool double stranded, work a large French knot for each eye and a few stitches for the nose.

Make a white pompon for the tail and sew it in position.

FINISHED MEASUREMENTS
Height Approx 40cm/16in

MATERIALS
Yarn Sublime Extra Fine Merino DK (100% merino wool, 116m/127yd):
2 x 50g/1¾oz balls shade Salty Grey (MC), 1 x 50g/1¾oz ball shade Miss Plum (CC), plus oddments of white, pink, black and green, and various colours as required for skirt
Needles 1 pair needles size 3.25mm (US3), 2 stitch holders or safety pins
Notions Toy-grade stuffing

TENSION (GAUGE)
Approx 24 sts and rows measure 10cm/4in over garter st on 3.25mm (US3) needles, although tension (gauge) is not too important for this project

'Marigold' Cat

Patterns for knitted toys from before 1940 are quite scarce. Those that do exist appear to be based on paper sewing patterns. They are often worked in garter stitch, the simplest stitch in which to reproduce various shapes. The original pattern for this toy cat was produced during the war when wool was rationed and so various oddments are recommended. The upper body is knitted in a different colour to resemble a sweater, but the skirt is knitted separately and then sewn on; if you want it to be removable, just put some elastic in the waist.

HEAD
Gusset
Using MC, cast on 7 sts and knit 10 rows, inc 1 st at each end of second and alt rows. *(17 sts)*
Work 30 rows without shaping.
Next row: Dec 1 st at each end of row. *(15 sts)*
Next row: Knit.
Rep these last 2 rows until 3 sts rem.
K3tog and fasten off.

Sides of head (make 2)
Using MC, cast on 12 sts and knit 10 rows.

Shape front of head
Row 1: Cast on 3 sts at beg of next row. *(15 sts)*
Row 2: K1, kfb in next st, k to end. *(16 sts)*
Row 3: K to last 2 sts, kfb in next st, k1. *(17 sts)*
Rep the last 2 rows once more. *(19 sts)*
Knit 20 rows without shaping.

Shape top of head
Row 1: K11, turn.
Row 2: K11.
Row 3: K13, turn.
Row 4: K13.

Row 5: K19.
Knit 9 rows, dec 1 st at end of every alt row. *(14 sts)*
Cast (bind) off.

Ear backs (make 2)
Using MC, cast on 16 sts.
Knit 2 rows.
Row 3: K2tog, k14. *(15 sts)*
Rows 4 and 5: Knit.
Row 6: K2tog, k11, k2tog. *(13 sts)*
Rows 7 and 8: Knit.
Row 9: K2tog, k11. *(12 sts)*
Rows 10 and 11: Knit.
Row 12: K2tog, k8, k2tog. *(10 sts)*

What the Children s

Rows 13 and 14: Knit.
Row 15: K2tog, k6, k2tog. (8 sts)
Row 16: K6, k2tog. (7 sts)
Row 17: K2tog, k3, k2tog. (5 sts)
Cast (bind) off, working k2tog at each end.

Ear fronts (make 2)
Using pink yarn, cast on 14 sts.
Row 1: Knit.
Row 2: Purl.
Cont in St st:
Row 3: K2tog, k to end. (13 sts)
Row 4: Purl.
Row 5: Knit.
Row 6: P2tog, p9, p2tog. (11 sts)
Row 7: Knit.
Row 8: Purl.
Row 9: K2tog, k to end. (10 sts)
Row 10: Purl.
Row 11: K2tog, k6, k2tog. (8 sts)
Row 12: Purl.
Row 13: [K2tog] to end. (4 sts)
Row 14: [P2tog] twice. (2 sts)
Row 15: K2tog and fasten off.

Body (including legs, make 2)
Using C, cast on 20 sts and work [k1, p1] rib for 6 rows.
Working in garter st (knit every row), cast on 5 sts at beg of next 2 rows. (30 sts)
Knit 36 rows.
Break C yarn and change to white.
Work 10 rows St st, inc 1 st at beg and end of next and every alt row to 40 sts.
Cont in St st without shaping for 10 more rows.

Divide for legs
Next row (RS): K20, turn.
Cont in St st on these 20 sts for 3 more rows.
Next row: K1, [k2tog] twice, k to end. (18 sts)

Next row: Purl.
Next row (RS): K1, [k2tog] twice, k8, [k2tog] twice, k1. (14 sts)
Work 3 rows St st.
Break white yarn and rejoin MC.
Knit 8 rows in garter st.
Row 9: K2tog, k10, k2tog. (12 sts)
Knit 3 rows.
Row 13: K2tog, k8, k2tog. (10 sts)
Knit 36 rows.
Knit 2 more rows, dec 1 st at each end. (6 sts)
Cast (bind) off.

Arms (make 2)
Using C, cast on 26 sts and knit 20 rows.
Dec 1 st at each end of next row. (24 sts)
Knit 18 rows.
Next row: [K1, k2tog] to end. (16 sts)
Break C yarn and join MC.
Knit 12 rows.
Knit 2 rows, dec 1 st at each end. (12 sts)
Cast (bind) off, working k2tog across row.

Tail
Using MC, cast on 20 sts and knit 76 rows.
Next row: [K2tog, k6, k2tog] twice. (16 sts)
Knit 6 rows, dec 1 st at each end of alt rows. (10 sts)
Next row: K2tog to end. (5 sts)
Next row: K2tog, k1, k2tog. (3 sts)
K3tog and fasten off.

Skirt
Using the main colour you have chosen for the skirt, cast on 60 sts and work 5 rows [k1, p1] rib.
Work 2 rows St st.
Next row (RS): [Kfb, k1] 30 times to 90 sts.
Cont in St st in whatever colours and/or stripe patt as desired until skirt

measures 10cm/4in.
Work 2 more rows St st, then 6 rows garter st for hem.
Cast (bind) off.

Finishing
Block pieces as given on page 142. Fold arm pieces in half and sew seam, leaving top open for stuffing. Place body pieces together and sew down sides of neck extension and shoulders. Leave enough space to insert top of arms and then sew rest of side seams of body. Sew across bottom of feet and inner seams of legs, leaving a space to insert stuffing. Stuff arms, body and legs. Sew remaining leg seam. Insert arms into armholes so that they don't stick out at right angles, and stitch them in place. If necessary, put more stuffing into top of body through hole at neck.

Head
Sew gusset to head sides with pointed part to front, and joining with side pieces in the nose area. Stuff head. Run a gathering stitch around neck edge. Place head over the top of the neck extension. Draw up the gathering thread so that the head fits snugly and sew the head securely into place. Sew fronts of ears to backs and stitch ears securely into place. Embroider features.

Tail
Sew seam of tail, stuff and sew in place.

Skirt
Sew back seam of skirt.
Sew skirt to waist.

FINISHED MEASUREMENTS
Each block 7.5 x 7.5 x 7.5cm/3 x 3 x 3in

MATERIALS
Yarn Approx 30g/1oz 4 ply yarn for each brick, changing colours as required; work each square in a different colour or the whole brick in one colour
Needles 1 pair needles size 3.25mm (US3), 1 stitch marker
Notions 7.5cm/3in cube of upholstery foam for each brick

TENSION (GAUGE)
28 sts and 28 rows measure 10cm/4in over garter st on 3.25mm (US3) needles (or size needed to obtain given tension/gauge)

'Snapdragon' Bricks

These bricks are soft enough to be thrown around but sturdy enough to be piled on top of one another. They are easy to make and are a colourful, versatile toy that all babies will love – you could add a little bell or rattle into the stuffing to make them even more appealing. Surprisingly, there are few patterns for knitted toys until the 1950s, when they began to be published in magazines, so I designed this one from scratch.

Blocks are worked as 6 mitred squares, with each square picking up sts from previous squares, and the seams knitted as you go.

First square
Using 3.25mm (US3) needles, cast on 40 sts, placing marker after 20 sts. Knit 1 row.

Start shaping
Row 1: K to 2 sts before marker, k2tog, sm, ssk, k to end. *(38 sts)*
Row 2: Knit.

Rep these 2 rows until 2 sts rem. K2tog and fasten off.

Second square
As first square.

Place these 2 squares side by side with their points touching and the first square on the right.

Third square
Pick up and knit 20 sts along left slope of first square.
Pick up and knit 20 sts along right slope of second square. *(40 sts)*
Cont as first square from row 2.

Fourth square
Pick up and knit 20 sts from edge of third square and 20 sts from edge of second square. *(40 sts)*
Complete as first square from row 2.

Fifth square
Pick up and knit 20 sts from edge of first square, and 20 sts from edge of third square. *(40 sts)*
Complete as first square, as before, but knit last stitch on RS rows together with edge st from fourth square, creating a knitted seam.

Sixth square
Pick up and knit 20 sts from edge of fifth square and 20 sts from edge of fourth square. *(40 sts)*
Complete as first square but knit last stitch on RS rows together with sts from cast-on row of second square.

Finishing
Insert foam block. Sew up rem 2 seams.

BRICK DIAGRAMS

Side 3

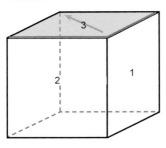

Side 4

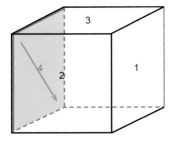

Side 5

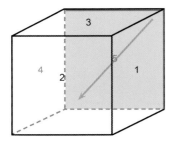

Side 6

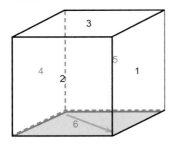

KEY

pick up sts

direction of knitting

Blocking

When you have finished knitting, the garment pieces have to be blocked and sewn together. Pin each garment piece out on a flat surface to the correct measurements. The blocking surface can be a firm base, such as the floor or a table covered with a blanket or towel, with a cotton sheet or a piece of checked cloth, which you can use as a guide to keep the edges straight, placed on top. Then lightly spray the knitting with cold, clean water until it is damp but not soaked, and leave it to dry naturally.

For cotton garments, pin out each piece to size and then lightly press them using a steam iron or a damp cloth and a regular iron. Do not move the iron across the fabric, as this will stretch it, but press it gently with up-and-down movements. Lace knitting is very delicate, but it does need careful blocking in order to obtain the openwork effect. In this case, lay the lace knitting on your blocking surface and dampen it lightly. Then very gently ease it to the correct shape and size, and leave it to dry naturally.

Abbreviations

alt	alternate
beg	beginning
CC	contrast colour
cm	centimetre(s)
cont	continue/continuing
dec	decrease/decreasing
foll	follows/following
in	inch(es)
inc	increase/increasing
k	knit
kfb	knit into the front and back of next stitch (increases by one stitch)
KLL	increase one st by knitting into left leg of st below first st on right-hand needle
k1US	knit one under strands – slip RH needle under loose strands and knit next st, lifting strands over the back of this stitch
k2tog	knit the next two sts together as one (decreases by one stitch)
LF	left front
MC	main colour
M1L	make one left – insert left-hand needle under bar between the 2 sts, from front to back, and knit into the back of it (increases by one stitch)
M1R	make one right – insert left-hand needle under bar between the 2 sts, from back to front, and knit into the front of it (increases by one stitch)
p	purl
patt	pattern
PLL	increase one st by purling into left leg of st below first st on right-hand needle
psso	pass slipped stitch over
p2tog	purl the next two sts together as one (decreases by one stitch)
rem	remain(s)/remaining
rep	repeat
RF	right front
rnd(s)	round(s)
RS	right side
sk2po	slip1, knit 2 together, psso
sl	slip
sm	slip marker
ssk	slip slip knit (slip next 2 sts knitwise, then insert left needle into the fronts and knit the 2 sts together through the back)
st(s)	stitch(es)
St st	stocking (stockinette) stitch
tbl	through the back loop
WS	wrong side
wyif	with yarn in front
w & t	wrap and turn
yb	yarn back
yf	yarn forward
yd	yard(s)
yo	yarn over
2/2 FC	slip next 2 sts onto cable needle and hold in front of work, knit the next 2 sts, then knit 2 sts from cable needle

Crochet abbreviations
Crochet terminology differs between the UK and the US. Both UK and US terms and abbreviations are included, with US terms given in parentheses in the patterns.

dc (sc)	double (single) crochet
ch	chain
htr (hdc)	half treble (half double)
tr (dc)	treble (double)

Resources

Alpaca Select
www.alpaca-select.co.uk

Artesano Yarns
www.artesanoyarns.co.uk

Baruffa Cashmere
www.toddshandknits.com

Blacker Swan
www.blackeryarns.co.uk

Brown Sheep Yarns
www.magpielly.co.uk

Debbie Bliss
www.designeryarns.uk.com

DMC
www.purplelindacrafts.co.uk

Drops
www.woolwarehouse.co.uk

Fyberspates
www.fyberspates.co.uk

Hjertegarn Yarns
www.artyarn.co.uk

Jamiesons of Shetland
www.jamiesonsofshetland.co.uk

Katia Yarns
www.blacksheepwools.com

King Cole Yarns
www.kingcole.co.uk

Knitting Fever
www.knittingfever.com

Patons Yarn
www.woolwarehouse.co.uk

Shilasdair
www.theskyeshilasdairshop.co.uk

Simply Ribbons
www.simplyribbons.com

Sirdar
www.sirdar.co.uk

Sublime Yarns
www.craftyewe.co.uk
www.sublimeyarns.com/yarns

Totally Buttons
www.totallybuttons.com

Wendy Yarns
www.tbramsden.co.uk

Acknowledgements

With many thanks to all at Jacqui Small Publishing who nursed this project through all its stages, especially Zia Mattocks and Claire Chandler, and to Sarah Rock, Polly Wreford, Deirdre Rooney and Isabel de Cordova for the lovely photographs. Thank you to Linda McCreadie, who has checked and tech-edited all the patterns.

Many thanks to my friends and neighbours who helped me to complete the garments: Hilary Grundy, Anne Humphrey, Audrey Lincoln, Brenda Tipple and Sue Wylie.

Thank you to Dorothy Redmond of the Crafty Ewe wool shop in Norwich, and to my husband, for his patience, enthusiasm and support while I have been working on this book.

The publisher would like to thank the following companies for their kind loan of additional clothes for photography:
The Little White Company
(www.thewhitecompany.com)
Lizzie's (71 Webb's Road, London SW11 6SD
+44 (0)20 7738 2973)
Mamas & Papas (www.mamasandpapas.com)
Petit Bateau (www.petit-bateau.co.uk)

Thank you to all of our gorgeous models:

Estelle Abberley, Orla Barnaville, Albie de Winton,
Arabella Duffy, Leo Flynn, Isabella Harris,
Emile Harvey, Amelia McKee and Finn Warren